C000274602

The Essential Guide to Welsh Heritage and Scenic Railways

by
Mervyn Jones

THE OAKWOOD PRESS

© Oakwood Press & Mervyn Jones 2010

British Library Cataloguing in Publication Data
A Record for this book is available from the British Library
ISBN 978 0 85361 702 0

Typeset by Oakwood Graphics.
Repro by pkmediaworks, Cranborne, Dorset.
Printed by Cambrian Printers Ltd, Aberystwyth, Ceredigeon.

About the Author

Mervyn Jones has had a lifetime interest in railways since the early 1950s when the former 'LMS' was his passion. After retiring from a long career in public service towards the end of 1997, he has spent much of his time with his wife in Europe and the Far East, spending some (a lot, his wife would say!) of their time studying and photographing railways in a number of countries. Their highlight beyond Europe was in 2002 to (Outer) Mongolia and China travelling there and back on the Trans-Siberian and Trans-Mongolian railways.

He is a keen photographer and is a member of the Royal Photographic Society. He has been awarded a Master of Science degree from Cranfield University and prior to writing books on European railways he published numerous articles on academic subjects as well as a book, converted from his MSc thesis, a socio-psychological study of organizational behaviour. He lives with his wife, Caroline, half of the year in their home in North Wales on the Shropshire and Cheshire borders and the other half in the south of France close to Avignon and Nîmes.

His previous railway publications were *The Essential Guide to French Heritage and Tourist Railways* (2006) and *The Essential Guide to Swiss Heritage and Tourist Railways* (2007), *The Essential Guide to Austrian Railways and Tramways* (2008) and *A Pictorial Guide to Alpine Railways* (2009) all published by The Oakwood Press.

Front cover: On 25th April, 2009 the South Devon Railway's 1928-built 2-6-2T No. 5526 with 1934-built GWR Collett prairie No. 5199 double-head a service towards Carrog on the Llangollen Railway. The train is captured here from a vantage point on the A5 trunk road about two miles east of Glyndyfrdwy station. *Author*

Title page: No. 7 *Tom Rolt* arriving at Brynglas on the Talyllyn Railway on 7th August, 2009. *Caroline Jones*

Rear cover: An Arriva service bound for Barmouth passes beneath Harlech Castle on 6th August, 2009. *Author*

Published by The Oakwood Press (Usk), P.O. Box 13, Usk, Mon., NP15 1YS.
E-mail: sales@oakwoodpress.co.uk
Website: www.oakwoodpress.co.uk

Contents

On 6th August, 2009 the West Coast Railway Company operated 'The Cambrian' steam special deploying BR Standard '4MT' class No. 76079 seen here, tender first, as it passes the beautiful but hardly-crowded beach north of Barmouth.   *Author*

Acknowledgements

The author acknowledges the help, support, advice and, indeed, friendship, he has received from many during the research, photography and later the writing of this guide. It is not practical to identify all those who helped by name but, nonetheless, their individual contributions are very much appreciated. Much of the information presented in this book has been gleaned from the many excellent webpages produced by the webmasters of the various railway organisations in Wales. The author has respected copyright issues but nonetheless where the website URL is identified in the text entry then full credit is automatically accorded as a source of information albeit the author in his writing may well have introduced his own style, imperfect as that may be! Notwithstanding the valued support given from all quarters, the responsibility for all errors and omissions rests with the author. The excellent assistance given by the main rail transport provider in Wales, Arriva Trains Wales and in particular their marketing department, is gratefully acknowledged. A special mention must also be given to the author's dear friends, Luned and Bob Jones of Builth Wells, who were most helpful in providing some instruction in Welsh. However, any errors found herein in the use of the language or in spelling are entirely the responsibility of the author. *Diolch yn fawr iawn.*

As with the earlier publications, the author thanks Jane Kennedy the proprietor of the Oakwood Press for her encouragement, and also to Ian Kennedy, for his patience, support, useful comments and helpful suggestions. The author is also appreciative of the meticulous efforts of the editor employed by the Oakwood Press. The author does not know his name, nor in writing the previous four books has he ever met him, so, to the author, he will always be known as 'The Stig' (with apologies to BBC's *Top Gear*).

Finally, the author gives special thanks to his wife, Caroline. Not only did she take many of the photographs included in this book, but also she uncomplainingly supported him throughout the project. She accompanied him on all the numerous site visits often patiently waiting, in all weathers, for yet another train to pass which they did not always do! During the writing up of the guide, she gave much needed encouragement and advice as well as helpful, critical appraisal of the text. The author's seven-year-old Jack Russell, *Taiga*, is also thanked for his patience sitting for hours in the car whilst 'mum' and 'dad' do their thing! Those keen-eyed readers of the author's previous books will be aware that *Taiga* regularly could be seen in some of the photographs, rather like Terence Cuneo's mouse! *Taiga* continues to make appearances in this book.

This book is dedicated to the author's uncle, Mr Allenby Brown of Chirk, North Wales and his late wife Rhoda, who gave much love and support to him during his early years. Allenby, now 90 years of age, continues to be a keen railway enthusiast.

Introduction

Welcome to Wales!

Where was the last foreign invasion onto British soil? Who was the last English king to be slain in battle and which Welsh-born was responsible for his death? Which Welsh church tower formed the model for the Victoria Tower at the Palace of Westminster? Where did the first meeting of the Women's Institute take place in Britain? In which city are Welshmen still under threat of decapitation by an unrepealed Royal Proclamation? Where is the smallest house in Great Britain? Many know of Wilfred Owen the World War I poet, but where was he born? Where is longest single-track railway tunnel in the United Kingdom? What is the 'electric mountain' and where is it in Wales? From where in Wales did flying boats operate during World War II? Where was the worst coal-mining disaster in British history? Where was the single factory employing the greatest number of workers ever in the United Kingdom? Where is the largest castle in Wales? To where, are three pilgrimages to a site in Wales the equivalent to one to Jerusalem? What is the longest monument in Britain? What is the 'Large Hadron Collider' and why is there a connection with a town in South Wales? What has been described as the 'largest, most fantastic bird table in the world'?

The answers to these questions and many more, perhaps unexpectedly, can be found in this publication. Information of this nature is an unlikely subject to feature in a book principally about railways. However, this is a book with a difference. In researching and writing about Welsh railways, the author, in addition to information about the prime subject matter, has chosen to include what he hopes are interesting facts about places and events close to where trains pass. In so doing, it is hoped that the book will enjoy a wider appeal than just for railway enthusiasts but should interest and inform the general holiday-maker and the traveller to beautiful Wales, a principality steeped in history and culture.

The book is the fifth Oakwood Press publication by the author on European railways and fourth in the Essential Guide series. The publication of the book has been timed to coincide with the anniversary of the founding, 175 years ago, of the Great Western Railway, a company which had a long association with the provision of railway services in Wales.

This guide lists a total of 62 locations throughout Wales (including five on the borders in England) where heritage and tourist railways and related activities can be found. A total of 163 photographs support the text. Those five just in England are justified for their close proximity to Wales and their relevance to the Welsh railway scene. Of the total locations, the author has identified 57 specific routes of which 28 are operated as heritage/tourist railways, including projects and societies, and 29 as regular rail service routes operated in Wales, mainly by Arriva Trains Wales but also by Virgin Trains, Cross Country Trains and First Great Western Trains. London Midland also runs trains in England close to the Welsh borders. Finally, there are five museums including two which are dedicated to the Great Western Railway, one being just over the border in England at Coleford in Gloucestershire and the other, also in England, at Swindon in Wiltshire. Wales is a popular destination for main line steam specials run by, for example West Coast Railway Company, Vintage Trains

Limited, Steam Dreams, Past Time Rail Ltd, Pathfinder Tours (2006) Ltd, PMR Tours and the Railway Touring Company. Some of these previous special excursions feature in this book.

An important question in writing a book such as this is what to include and what to exclude. Heritage and tourist-focused railways are, relatively speaking, easy to identify. However, where do regular service routes qualify as being of 'tourist' or 'scenic' interest especially as many areas in Wales were previously heavily industrialized with coal mining and steel production for example? Fortunately many of these areas, the Valleys in South Wales being a good case in point, have recovered by returning, what was previously derelict land, back to nature. This change is perhaps best summed up by a poem written by the children of Waunlwyd School for the Ebbw Fawr Mining Memorial which stands alongside the railway at Cwm.

> The grass is greener
> The rivers are cleaner
> It is so nice to see colour again
> The Miners were working
> So hard and we appreciate
> What they have done
> Now they can rest at long last,
> In a valley that is
> Cleaner and greener

How true! Given the outstanding natural beauty of Wales, therefore, very few routes fail to qualify in some way as is best evidenced perhaps by the photographs depicted in this book. It is hoped that the reader and visitor to Wales agrees. Enjoy the journey!

Talyllyn about to leave Brynglas on 7th August, 2009.   *Caroline Jones*

Chapter One

Getting the best out of this guide

To assist the reader in navigating his or her way to the 62 locations identified in this guide they have been laid out in the order of an imaginary journey, zigzagging, if one likes, across Wales. Beginning near the author's home at Wrexham in north-east Wales, the traveller goes up to Chester and then runs west across the northern part of the country to Llandudno, Bangor and the Isle of Anglesey passing other railways on the way. The traveller then moves east over to Llangollen and Oswestry and then returns west again to the coast near Barmouth and Aberystwyth. The journey continues down to south-west Wales and back along the coast to Cardiff, Newport and Chepstow and the border with England. Each railway/route has been awarded a unique numeric reference and where appropriate cross-references are applied to assist finding related information and nearby railways.

As was the case with the previous guide, the Alps, the content has been written in such a way as to appeal hopefully to a wider audience than just the die-hard railway enthusiast. This book, therefore, may frustrate the latter, although it is hoped that the pictorial aspects will satisfy many. To assist those who would wish to gain more information, there are a number of suggestions. Firstly, there are many other books which can help and some of these are shown in the Bibliography. Secondly, the internet increasingly is a quickly-accessed source of comprehensive information; to help in this respect relevant websites are identified in the text. This book includes a general list of websites which the author has found useful together with a record of railway related organisations and their addresses.

Welsh as a language is increasing in popularity of use - over 20 per cent of the population in Wales speak the language. To help, some English words in the text are given with their Welsh equivalent in parentheses. There is also a Glossary of some common railway and related terms in Welsh again presented with their English equivalent. Also included are a list of Welsh place names where railways operate. It will be seen many differ significantly from the English equivalents, e.g. *Abertawe* for Swansea.

Much effort has gone into ensuring that all the information in this guide is correct and up-to-date. This desire to ensure accuracy included writing to all the heritage/tourist railways and sending an extract of the Introduction together with the section of the book as it relates to the relevant organization. Most have responded and have provided the author with helpful comments and corrections, for which he is most grateful. It is important, however, to render a health warning. There are many changing factors particularly in heritage and tourist railway operations, short of closure or suspension, which can alter the availability of a service, not least of all the condition of many of the ageing locomotives and other rolling stock. In addition, much preserved railway material can and does move around Wales and sometimes England and Scotland. Before travelling any distance to any of the locations listed herein, therefore, it is sensible, in order to avoid disappointment, to check the state of current operations. Fortunately, the larger operators all have websites which it is hoped are maintained up to date. As far as regular services are concerned it should be noted that invariably there are reduced services on Saturdays and Sundays. On some lines no services run at all on Sundays but where limited services do operate these are sometimes substituted by bus services to allow engineering works to take place. However, such information can invariably be found in bulletins published on the internet.

Another issue of particular importance is, having seen something of interest in this book, how does the would-be visitor find it? For each of the 62 separate entries, the main towns through which the railways travel are listed; these should help the reader, using other sources, to identify the exact locations. In writing this book, the author gave much thought as to whether to make available maps for each of the entries or collections of them. The priority of this publication however, from the outset, has been to present a pictorial essay about Wales and its railways with supporting text. The limitations of space therefore, and the fact that the author is not a cartographer, have combined to exclude, what many might otherwise criticise as inadequate, detailed local maps were they to have been provided. However, the good news is that Arriva Trains Wales has come to the rescue by allowing the author to reproduce their excellent map of their rail network on which he has been allowed to superimpose the numeric references of the heritage railways and museums (*see page 21*). To help, the author has also identified Ordnance Survey (OS) grid references to the nearest location. Relevant OS maps are listed in the Bibliography. A very useful website to help the journey planner can be found at http://www.streetmap.co.uk

With the increasing popularity of mobile GPS devices, new to this particular Essential Guide is the provision of GPS coordinates for the prime locations listed. These hopefully will be some compensation for the absence of detailed maps for each railway. Google Earth™ on the Internet will assist the planner as it did the author.

Given the book is intended to help not just the railway enthusiast, a list of all the Tourist Information Centres in Wales, their locations and relevant e-mail addresses is included.

An alphabetical index is also provided linking to the unique reference numbers and, where appropriate, to page numbers.

Every attempt has been made to give as much as information as is possible in a book of this size and type. However, it is inevitable, given the enormity of the subject addressed, that it has only been possible to scratch the surface. This book is not an encyclopaedia. Hopefully, though, what the reader sees and reads here will whet the appetite to explore further. In other words, this book is only the start of an enjoyable railway journey through the outstandingly beautiful Wales and by no means its conclusion.

Safe journey!

Mervyn Jones
North Wales
May 2010

Chapter Two

The Geography of Wales

Wales consists of a peninsula in the central-west of Great Britain together with certain offshore islands of which by far the largest is Anglesey. As a separate country within the United Kingdom it has borders only with England to the east. It is surrounded by sea on the other three sides; the Bristol Channel to the south, St George's Channel to the west, and the Irish Sea to the north. The country is about 170 miles long and 60 miles wide and has a total surface of 8,023 square miles. It has over 746 miles of coastline. Much of Wales is mountainous distributed in three main regions. Snowdonia in the north-west, the Cambrians in mid-Wales and the Brecons to the south. The highest mountain in Wales is Snowdon standing at 3,560 ft (1,085 m.) and there are a further 13 (some say 14) peaks over 3,000 ft (914 m.) known as the Welsh 3,000s. Land use in Wales is distributed as follows: crops and fallow land three per cent, grassland and rough grazing 73 per cent, forest and woodland 13 per cent, urban development 10 per cent and other agricultural land one per cent.

Wales is divided into 22 unitary authorities, which are responsible for the provision of all local government services, including education, social work, environment and road services. There are what is referred to as the eight 'preserved counties' of Wales which are used for ceremonial purposes of the Lord Lieutenancy (HM Queen's representative) and Shrievalty (the High Sheriffs). The eight are almost identical with those counties that existed in 1996 before local government changes, i.e. Gwent, South Glamorgan, Mid-Glamorgan, West Glamorgan, Dyfed, Powys, Gwynedd and Clwyd. There are five cities in Wales: Cardiff (the capital), Swansea, Newport, St David's and Bangor. The main population and industrial areas in Wales are in the south, i.e. the Valleys and the cities of Cardiff, Swansea and Newport. A large proportion of the Welsh population live in small settlements with nearly 20 per cent inhabiting villages of less than 1,500 persons, which compares with 10 per cent in England. Wales has 26 per cent of its population living in large settlements of 100,000 or more compared with almost 40 per cent in England. The population of Wales according to the statistics published in 2009 was 2.98 million representing about five per cent of the overall United Kingdom population.

It is stated by the Welsh Assembly Government that well over a half million individuals can speak Welsh representing 20.5 per cent of the resident population. Between 1991 and 2001 there was an increase in the number of Welsh speakers in 14 of the 22 unitary authorities with a significant rise amongst schoolchildren. The popularity of education through the medium of Welsh has expanded since the first local authority primary school opened in Llanelli in 1947. This increase is not surprising given that about 20 per cent of primary school children now receive their education primarily in Welsh, including over 30 per cent in Wales's capital city, Cardiff. Incidentally, the University of Wales, Lampeter offer courses in Welsh by way of a residential course or by distanced learning at home/work (http://welsh.lamp.ac.uk).

Wales has three National Parks, i.e. the Snowdonia National Park which was the first to be designated in 1951, the Pembrokeshire Coast National Park along the Pembrokeshire coast (designated in 1952) and the Brecon Beacons (designated in 1957). The largest natural lakes in Wales are Bala Lake near Llangollen followed by Llangorse Lake, near Brecon. There are many man-made reservoirs, the largest being in the Elan Valley (including the Claerwen), Lake Vyrnwy, the Talybont Reservoir, and Llyn Brianne.

There is said to be a traditional list of seven geographic and cultural landmarks making up the 'Seven Wonders of Wales'. These are Snowdon, of course; the peal of bells in the medieval church of All Saints' at Gresford, near Wrexham; the Llangollen bridge over the River Dee built in 1347; the oldest continuously operating pilgrimage site of St Winefride's Well at Holywell in Flintshire; the tower on the 16th century Church of St Giles in Wrexham; the ancient yew trees, said to be 1,500-2,000 years old, in the churchyard of St Mary's at Overton-on-Dee; and, the 240 ft waterfall called *Pistyll Rhaeadr* near Llanrhaeadr-ym-Mochnant in Powys, 12 miles west of Oswestry.

Tourism is big business in Wales and as a consequence the visitor will invariably be given a warm welcome. It is estimated that tourists spend on average over £8 million each day on trips in Wales, amounting to around £3 billion a year. Heritage and scenic railways play an important part in generating that income.

Snowdon as seen from the platform of Talsarnau station on 25th January, 2009.

Caroline Jones

Chapter Three

A Brief History of Wales

It was probably the establishment of a border between England and Wales by the digging of a dyke on the instructions of King Offa of Mercia in the 8th century which saw the beginnings of Wales as a nation. Earlier victories by the Anglo-Saxons at Bath in 577 and at Chester in 613 had pushed the Celtic tribes to the western peninsula where they were protected by the Welsh mountains. Wales derives its name from the Anglo-Saxon word *wealas* which meant 'foreigners'. For the isolated Celts themselves they began to refer to themselves as *cymry* meaning fellow-countrymen and called their territory the now familiar *Cymru*.

By the middle of the 9th century the Welsh tribes had begun to develop into something resembling a cohesive nation. This was often achieved by the outcomes of various battles between tribes as well as marriages between powerful families. The success of Rhodri Mawr (w. *Rhodri ap Merfyn*) as a powerful unifying force meant that he had become the 'King' of most of the region by the time of his death at the age of 58 years. Wales was under constant threat from Viking invasions from across the Irish Sea, Dublin being their base. Rhodri Mawr derived much of his prestige by being a successful warrior especially against the Vikings who focused many of their attacks on the peoples of the Isle of Anglesey. In 856 Rhodri won a great victory on the island over Horn, the leader of the Danes. It was not only from the west that Rhodri was under threat: the English in the Kingdom of Mercia also posed danger especially in Powys where he had become ruler by inheriting his mother's land. Indeed it was at a battle on this frontier in 878 that Rhodri and his son Gwriad were killed.

However, the most sustained threat to the independence of the Welsh tribes began after the Norman Conquest and again it came from the east. By this time Wales was organized into four principalities: Gwynedd in the north, Powys in the south, Deheubarth in the south-west and Morgannwg in the south-east. After the Battle of Hastings in 1066, William the Conqueror made no attempt to take Wales. Instead he gave earldoms to his key supporters, for the regions of Chester, Shrewsbury and Hereford. These earls, or marcher lords (derived from the word 'march' meaning border), were renowned for their violence towards the Welsh. Unfortunately for the Welsh, there was no serious resistance for the *cymry* were often still at war between themselves. However, by the 13th century, successive rulers from the royal family of Gwynedd had managed to unify Wales and were generally accepted as overall rulers. The first was Llywelyn ab Iorwerth who, on his death in 1240, was chronicled as the 'Prince of Wales'. He was succeeded by his son, David II, who claimed the title as his own. In 1244, David's nephew, Llywelyn ap Gruffudd, secured the approval of Baron Simon de Montfort and later the authority of the English King Henry III to use the title Prince of Wales, as was ratified by the Treaty of Montgomery in 1267.

Conwy Castle, built by Edward I, photographed on a bright day in early March 2010.   *Author*

Church of St Giles in Wrexham.   *Author*

This formal recognition was short-lived for, after Henry III's death, his eldest son, Edward I (known as 'longshanks' due to his great height) came to the English throne. The English-Welsh relationship deteriorated from then on brought about largely by Llywelyn ap Gruffudd (sometimes spelt Gruffydd). He failed to attend Edward's coronation, declined a summons to do homage and refused to discharge a large debt he owed the English king. Edward, a much more aggressive man than his father, moved decisively. He sent three English armies into Wales from Chester, Shrewsbury and Hereford to impose his rule. Eventually Llywelyn and his forces were isolated in Snowdonia and compelled to surrender, signing a treaty at Conwy Castle which effectively stripped him of much of his territory.

The king ordered that most of Wales thereafter be administered by English agents who, as it turned out, fulfilled their duties diligently, indeed often brutally. This led to an uprising which was put down by another invasion by Edward's forces and in which Llywelyn was killed. The whole of Wales was then assumed by the king as ratified by a statute issued at Rhuddlan Castle in 1284. The effect of this Act was to divide Wales into counties resembling the English model which were to be governed by officials of the Crown. To add insult to the injury, in 1301 Edward revived the title of 'Prince of Wales', much cherished by the Welsh, and bestowed it on his heir, the future Edward II. The title has remained down the centuries, the highest honour granted to the eldest son and heir apparent of the monarch. The year after the Llywelyn's death, as part of his policy of ensuring obedience, Edward set about the construction of great castles. Each completed within a matter of a few years, they formed what some called an 'iron ring' around the last Welsh refuge, Snowdonia. Today these castles, Conwy, Harlech, Caernarfon and Beaumaris have all survived. The impact of these structures was to subdue and contain the Welsh for over a century and until such a time as Owain Glyn Dŵr arrived on the scene.

Ruling England from 1377 to 1399 was Richard II, who is perhaps best remembered for suppressing the Peasants' Revolt. He had no son and therefore during his reign there was no Prince of Wales. The end came for Richard when Henry IV seized the English throne in 1399 and established his son Henry as the Prince of Wales. The following year the Welsh proclaimed their own Prince of Wales, Owain Glyn Dŵr.

It was a deliberate act of rebellion. Under Glyn Dŵr's leadership the uprising grew in spite of an early defeat at Welshpool in 1400. Success for the rebels came with the capture, two years later, of Edmund Mortimer, member of an Anglo-Norman family with large estates on the Welsh borders. Mortimer was related by descent to the English throne and by marriage to the Percy family, the Earls of Northumberland. Glyn Dŵr managed to persuade Mortimer to change sides. Mortimer later married Glyn Dŵr's daughter, Catrin. Henry IV now faced serious, indeed dangerous opposition, with the Earl of Northumberland able to raise the North of England against him aided by Mortimer and Glyn Dŵr with much of the West of England and Wales in opposition. The death of Henry Percy, known as 'Hotspur', at the Battle at Shrewsbury in 1403, was a hindrance for the rebels. However, in 1404, Glyn Dŵr captured Aberystwyth and Harlech and began to rule as the Prince of Wales, establishing an administration,

Aberystwyth town as seen from the castle grounds.   *Caroline Jones*

The waterfront at Cardiff Bay with the glass-fronted Welsh Assembly building standing to the right.   *Author*

The Memorial to Owain Glyn Dŵr sited in Corwen town. There is also a sculpture of Glyn Dŵr by Alfred Turner displayed in the City Hall at Cardiff.
Author

holding parliaments, negotiating with the Pope about the appointment of Welsh bishops and so on. In 1405, buoyed by success, an alliance was drawn up between himself, Mortimer and Northumberland as to how they would subsequently carve up England and Wales between themselves. However, the success was not to last as from that year onwards matters turned against them as a result of the persistent counter-efforts of the other Prince of Wales who was later to become Henry V. In 1408, Glyn Dŵr lost Aberystwyth and Harlech and by 1410 his status had been reduced to that of an outlaw. After 1412 no more was heard of him and it is believed he may well have died somewhere in hiding about 1416.

Wales yet again had failed to achieve their own Welsh Prince of Wales. However, fortunes changed, when, in 1485, Henry Tudor, a 'Welshman' born in Pembroke Castle, killed King Richard III on the battlefield and became King Henry VII of England and Wales. The effect of this accession was to change the status of Wales from being a conquered territory to being an integral part of the English kingdom as formalized in a series of laws enacted between 1536 and 1543. This Act of Union, as it later became known, meant that Wales was given an administrative system based on counties, the right to be represented in the English parliament and the status of principality within the combined kingdom. The downside for many was that English, not Welsh, was decreed to be the first language of the country, a change that is still resented by many in Wales today. Henry VII died in 1509 and was succeeded by his second son, Henry VIII. From that time on in what was the period of the Reformation and beyond, the histories of the two countries, generally speaking, have run in tandem.

Perhaps the most significant change politically since those earlier times occurred towards the end of the 20th century when certain powers were devolved to Scotland, Northern Ireland and Wales. The 60-seat Welsh Assembly was officially opened on 26th May, 1999. It is housed in a purpose-built building on the Cardiff Bay complex.

A memorial to Trevithick's steam locomotive standing in Merthyr Tydfil close to where it first ran in 1804.   *Author*

Chapter Four

A Brief History of Railways in Wales

In 1804 the first steam railway locomotive was introduced by Cornwall-born Richard Trevithick (1771-1833). In 1799, he had been the first engineer to successfully build a high pressure stationary steam engine. He followed this in 1801 by constructing a steam carriage for use on the roads but this innovation ended in failure. Perhaps his most important achievement was when he built the steam locomotive for the narrow gauge rails on the Merthyr Tydfil Tramroad, sometimes referred to as the Penydarren Tramroad. The locomotive used a high pressure cylinder without a condenser, the exhaust steam being used to assist the draught via the firebox, thus increasing efficiency. These improvements in Trevithick's steam engine designs amazingly did not change for the duration of the steam era. Amid great interest from the public, on 21st February, 1804, the locomotive successfully moved 10 tons of iron, five wagons and 70 men a distance of 9¾ miles from Penydarren to Abercynon. The journey took four hours and five minutes at an average speed of nearly 2½ mph. The locomotive had proved that steam traction had a future. However, the use of this particular Trevithick locomotive did not last as it was found to be too heavy for the primitive track, as was a second one he built for the Wylam colliery in County Durham.

The first passenger railway service is said to be the Mumbles Tram and operated for the first time in March 1807. On the instigation of Benjamin French, a carriage was converted to carry passengers. It was pulled by a horse between the dunes at Swansea to Mumbles, an oyster harvesting and fishing village on the west of the bay. The service ran in many guises until its closure in January 1960 much to the consternation of local residents. For more on the history of the Mumbles Tram visit the website www.welshwales.co.uk/mumbles_railway_swansea.htm

From the early part of the 19th century there was rapid expansion in the construction of railways. The Great Western Railway was created by Act of Parliament on 31st August, 1835. However there were many more, invariably small individual companies, meeting local needs. The Cambrian Railways, for example, between 1864 and 1904 took over the Oswestry & Newtown Railway (established 1860), the Llanidloes & Newtown Railway (1853), the Newtown & Machynlleth Railway (1857), the Oswestry, Ellesmere & Whitchurch Railway (1861), the Aberystwyth & Welsh Coast Railway (1861) and the Mid-Wales Railway (1859). The Festiniog [sic] Railway carried slate from 1836 and passengers from 1865. The Llanelly [sic] Railway & Dock Company was incorporated in 1828, the Rhymney Railway in 1854 and the Taff Vale Railway (TVR) in 1836. Eight railways were amalgamated with the TVR including the Aberdare Railway which had opened in 1846. Many more companies came and went and are too numerous to list here. Fortunately for those who wish to take their enquiries further, the history of many these has been recorded for posterity in a wealth of publications many of which have been published by the the the Oakwood Press.

Conwy Castle with its railway bridge, which is a wrought-iron tubular bridge built by Robert Stephenson in 1848. Whilst passing through the bridge trains are completely out of sight, as was the case here on 2nd August, 2009. On the far side of the railway bridge is the Conwy suspension road bridge which was built in 1826 by Thomas Telford, replacing a ferry that once operated at that point. The bridge was one of the world's first road suspension bridges but it now may only be crossed on foot; it is in the care of the National Trust and open from mid-March to October. The bridge's supporting towers which can just about be seen were designed to complement the castle's turrets. *Author*

Pannier tank No. 6430 caught at Berwyn station on the Llangollen Railway on 25th March, 2006. *Author*

By the end of World War I in spite of many amalgamations there were still too many railway companies, 120 in fact, distributed throughout Wales and the rest of Britain, many of which were making huge losses. As a consequence it was the Government led by a Welshman, Prime Minister David Lloyd George, which enacted the Railway Act of 1921. It was also known as the Grouping Act which gives a clue as to its purpose.

The opening paragraph of the Act stated:

With a view to the reorganisation and more efficient and economical working of the railway system of Great Britain railways shall be formed into groups in accordance with the provisions of this Act, and the principal railway companies in each group shall be amalgamated, and other companies absorbed in manner provided by this Act.

The Act came into effect at the beginning of 1923. The new companies, the 'Big Four' as they became to be known, were the London, Midland & Scottish Railway (LMS), the London & North Eastern Railway (LNER), the Southern Railway (SR) and the expanded Great Western Railway (GWR). The GWR was already a long established company that linked London with the south and west of England and much of Wales. It had been founded in 1833 and provided for by statute in 1835. It ran its first trains three years later. It was built by one of Britain's greatest engineers Isambard Kingdom Brunel who chose a broad gauge of 7 ft 1¼ in. However, from 1854, following a series of take-overs, the GWR was also operating on standard gauge track of 4 ft 8½ in. Broad gauge did not win the 'battle of the gauges', the last such line ending in 1892. The GWR was the only company to keep its name following the 1921 Railways Act which it retained until 1948 when the company was nationalized. It then became the Western Region of British Railways. The GWR was called by some 'God's Wonderful Railway' and by others the 'Great Way Round'. It was also known as the 'holiday line' taking many people to resorts in the West Country. Whatever memories people have, it was still a great railway.

The GWR locomotives, many of which were built in Swindon, were painted in a Brunswick green colour, and its carriages were resplendent in 'chocolate and cream' livery. Wagons were initially painted red but this later was changed to a mid-grey. GWR ran suburban and rural services as well as long-distance express trains such as the 'Flying Dutchman' (in broad gauge days), the 'Cornish Riviera Express' and the 'Cheltenham Spa Express'. The company did not restrict its operations to the railways. A network of bus routes was provided and ships, docks and hotels were also owned.

There was initially no direct line from London to Wales as the River Severn was considered too wide to cross. Consequently, trains had to follow an otherwise longer route by way of Gloucester where the river was narrow enough to be crossed by a bridge. This was costly and unsatisfactory for the GWR so work on a Severn Tunnel began in 1873 and was completed in 1886.

Nearly 50 years after nationalization British Railways, by then British Rail, was privatized. Part of the original GWR name was revived in a new company, Great Western Trains, and which was superseded by the current operator, First Great Western. Cross Country Trains also run in parts of Wales as do Virgin

On 27th February, 2010 a First Great Western service from Cardiff is about to disappear into the Severn Tunnel. The two lines to the right take trains to Chepstow and beyond. The rather untidy view is caused by the alterations currently being undertaken to modify the layout of the routes.
Author

Arriva's service to Holyhead, with dmu No. 175107 captured west of Abergele on 2nd August, 2009.   *Author*

ARRIVA Trains Wales
Trenau Arriva Cymru
© 2008 Arriva Trains Wales as amended

Trains with London Midland and Northern Trains both operating on or close to the borders.

By far the biggest operator in Wales is Arriva Trains Wales (ATW). This company is part of the Arriva Group, a leading provider of passenger transport throughout Europe. To provide rail services ATW has a fleet of 125 trains covering routes totalling over 1,009 miles and employs a workforce of 2,050 persons. It operates 955 services each day which amount to 13.7 million miles travelled each year. On average, ATW handle around 65,000 passenger journeys a day and has the ability to carry over 12,000 customers at any one time. A total of 244 stations are operated throughout England and Wales of which 53 are currently staffed. The railway enthusiast can learn more by visiting www.arrivatrainswales.co.uk/Rail_Enthusiasts2.aspx Arriva also operate extensive bus services throughout Wales.

The operating infrastructure for ATW, i.e. the rail network, was transferred to a separate agency, Railtrack, in 1994 and eight years later to a new enterprise, Network Rail. Where possible, much has been done to preserve stations (or parts of them), signal boxes and bridges allowing one to still see historic GWR structures in operation on a modern network. All service trains in Wales operate on the standard 4 ft 8½ in. gauge track. There are no rail routes which have benefited from electrification in Wales, although in 2009 the Government announced that it intended to electrify the Great Western main line to Swansea.

Great Little Trains of Wales

The *Great Little Trains of Wales* promotion is a very special way of seeing some of the best scenery in the British Isles. All 10 'little trains' listed are narrow gauge steam railways which have been identified in the book, viz. Talyllyn (*see entry 26*), Llanberis Lake Railway (*see entry 21*), Ffestiniog Railway (*see entry 18*), Welsh Highland Railway (*see entry 19*), Welshpool & Llanfair Railway (*see entry 32*), Vale of Rheidol (*see entry 30*), Brecon Mountain Railway (*see entry 50*), Bala Lake Railway (*see entry 17*), Welsh Highland Heritage Railway (*see entry 20*) and the Snowdon Mountain Railway (*see entry 22*). *Great Little Trains of Wales* offers a discount card which for £10 entitles the holder to 20 per cent off one adult full round trip fare on normal timetabled trains on the participating railways as listed above and on the card. Discount cards are valid for 12 months from the date of the first journey. There are also discounts for *Great Little Trains of Wales* card holders in selected accommodation close to many of the member railways For more information, write to The Secretary, Great Little Trains of Wales, FREEPOST CS1226, Wharf Station, Tywyn, Gwynedd, LL36 9BR, or telephone 01654 710472 or visit the website www.greatlittletrainsofwales.co.uk

Chapter Five

The Railways

1 Wrexham and to the South

Locations: Wrexham and Shrewsbury.

GPS: Wrexham: 53°2′48.91″N 2°59′30.17″W. Shrewsbury 52°42′2.48″N 2°45′23.44″W.

OS map reference: Wrexham: SJ333499 Shrewsbury: SJ492124.

Operators: Arriva Trains Wales and Wrexham & Shropshire Railway.

Timetable: Arriva No. 4.

Arriva Route: Wrexham to Shrewsbury via Ruabon, Chirk and Gobowen (in Shropshire, England) with a journey time of 38 minutes and services every two hours.

Wrexham & Shropshire Route: Wrexham to London Marylebone via Ruabon, Chirk and into England at Gobowen, then Shrewsbury, Telford, Tame Bridge Parkway, Leamington Spa and Banbury with a journey time of just under four hours. There are four services each way each day. Off-peak economy fares are as low as £10 (2010) for a single journey to or from London if booked in advance. (See http://ticketing.wrexhamandshropshire.co.uk/best-value-tickets.php)

Websites: www.arrivatrainswales.co.uk www.wrexhamandshropshire.co.uk

History: The route, sometimes called the Severn-Dee Line (after the rivers on which the cities of Shrewsbury and Chester stand), was built in 1846 as the Shrewsbury & Chester Railway. The engineer for the line was Henry Robertson and the contractor was Thomas Brassey in partnership with William Mackenzie

An Arriva train crosses Cefn viaduct on 6th January, 2010 heading for Wrexham. The viaduct was built by Thomas Brassey in 1848 to the plans of Henry Robertson. The latter also constructed the nearby Chirk viaduct. *Author*

23

On 11th February, 2010 Arriva's class '175' No. 175115 crosses a girder bridge over the River Dee in Chester where the disaster occurred in 1847. The large expanse to the right is Chester's racecourse, the Roodee.   *Author*

The Pontcysyllte aqueduct high above the River Dee as photographed on 24th January, 2010 with the narrow boat *Shush* heading for the Trevor Basin.   *Author*

and Robert Stephenson, the son of George. Sadly, there was a disaster on the line in May 1847 when a local train to Ruabon carrying 22 passengers fell through the bridge into the River Dee resulting in five deaths and nine serious injuries. The bridge had been designed by Robert Stephenson who at the local inquest had been accused of negligence. The cause was found to be excessive weight on the bridge caused by the added weight of the train on the extensive ballasting previously placed on the wooden structure. The ballast was there to prevent the bridge catching fire. Stephenson had taken this precaution because he was aware of a fire on the Great Western Railway at Uxbridge when a bridge built by Isambard Kingdom Brunel had caught fire and collapsed.

Railway constructions of interest: Chirk and Cefn viaducts. Best viewed from the T Mawr Country Park, is the Cefn viaduct (GPS: 52°59′6.29″N 3°3′54.83″W), built by Thomas Brassey to carry the Shrewsbury & Chester Railway. It took two years to build at a cost of £72,346. It is 1,508 ft long, 147 ft high, and has 19 stone arches. The first public train, with 20 carriages, crossed the viaduct on 12th October, 1848.

What to see locally: The Pontcysyllte aqueduct (GPS: 52°58′15.17″N 3°5′28.99″W) carrying the Llangollen Canal over River Dee, between the villages of Trevor and Froncysyllte, is a must-see. If one has a head for heights, a walk along the towpath offers superb views of the River Dee, meandering through the meadows 123 ft below. The canal took Thomas Telford and William Jessop (an experienced canal engineer) 10 years to build and was completed in 1805. It is the longest - 998 ft 9 in. - and highest aqueduct in Great Britain. It is a Grade I listed building and, since 2009, a UNESCO World Heritage Site. Well worth a visit is Chirk Castle located on a nearby hilltop with stunning views over the Ceiriog valley to the south. It is believed that it was built by Roger Mortimer who was granted the lands by Edward I after defeating the Welsh in 1282. It is now in the ownership of the National Trust. Incidentally, the author's great, great grandfather, 'Ned King' was the chief ostler to the castle's previous owners, the Myddleton family. He was christened Edward Jones but throughout his working life was known to have a special way with horses earning the nomenclature Edward 'King of the Horses' Jones. In typical Welsh style his name was shortened. Also of interest are the ancient yew trees, said to be between 1,500-2,000 years old, in the churchyard of St Mary's at Overton-on-Dee, five miles east of Ruabon. The tower on the 16th century Church of St Giles in Wrexham is one of the Seven Wonders of Wales and is believed to have been a model for the Victoria Tower on London's Palace of Westminster (Houses of Parliament). Cefn Mawr, not far from Wrexham, is said to be the most haunted village in the whole of Europe. There are, whether you believe it or not, more than 75 ghost sightings every day in the village with the viaduct being a particularly popular haunt for ghosts from all over the Wrexham and nearby Cheshire areas!

Near to Offa's Dyke at Chirk, is the scene of a bloody battle between the Welsh and the English where stands the 'Great Oak', a penduculate oak, with a girth of 31 ft 3 in. The oak, sited on private land known as the Gate of the Dead near Chirk, is believed to be 1,200 years old. According to legend it is said that it was in 1165 that King Henry II, preparing to meet Owain Gwynedd for what became

A Wrexham and Shropshire train from London Marylebone heading for Wrexham crosses the Chirk viaduct on 20th July, 2009. The viaduct was built by the Scottish Engineer Henry Robertson between 1846 and 1848. A distance of 29 ft below the viaduct is the aqueduct carrying the Llangollen Canal which was constructed by Thomas Telford between 1796 and 1801.

Author

Chirk station platforms which will be the focus of a Glyn Valley Tramway project to produce a modern operating replica of the brick-built station. Chirk currently has two stone-built semi-open shelters as seen here on 13th February, 2009. *Author*

the Battle of Crogen, commanded his men to clear Ceiriog Woods to facilitate combat but ordered that the Great Oak be spared. However, the latest understanding is that the winter snows of 2010 have killed the tree by splitting the trunk down the middle.

Neighbouring railways: Llangollen Railway, Cambrian Heritage Railways at Llynclys and Oswestry and the Glyn Valley Tramway.

2 Glyn Valley Tramway

Locations: Chirk and Glyn Ceiriog.
GPS: Chirk: 52°55′52.27″N 3°3′22.68″W. Glyn Ceiriog: 52°55′53.83″N 3°11′19.44″W.
OS map references: Chirk: SJ284381. Glyn Ceiriog: SJ203382.
Operator: Glyn Valley Tramway Trust.
Contact details: Glyn Valley Tramway Trust, Pentre Garth, Pentre Cilgwyn, Llwynmawr, Wrexham LL20 7BG.
E-mail: The secretary is on gillpierce@yahoo.co.uk and the Chairman on david.pentregarth@hotmail.co.uk NB: These are the up-to-date e-mail addresses, those on the website no longer apply.
Gauge: Narrow (2 ft 6 in.). NB: The original gauge of the tramway was 2 ft 4½ in.
Website: www.glynvalleytramway.co.uk
Operating dates: Yet to be determined.
History of the Tramway: The Ceiriog Valley has an interesting industrial history as a result of the mining of local granite and slate as well as other local industries which operated in the valley. Originally material was moved with the aid of pack horses but this was overtaken eventually by mechanization with the construction of a tramway in 1873. With the arrival of steam traction the transportation developed with mixed trains of slate and other mineral products as well as some passenger services. An idea of what it was like to travel on this tramway is given by Glyn Valley Tramway Trust on their website: 'On the journey passengers would catch glimpses of the River Ceiriog running alongside the track. When the train reached Pontfadog many passengers would take the liberty of expecting the train to wait for them while they enjoyed a drink at the Swan Inn. Often the last customers emerging from the inn would have to dash across the road and would only just manage to clamber aboard in time before the train continued along its way to Dolywern and then onto Glyn Ceiriog'. The last tram ran on the line in 1935. Although it is 75 years since it last operated it is amazing how much of the old tramway has escaped the ravages of nature. Whilst road widening schemes have caused most of the trackbed alongside the B4500 road to have been lost, evidence of the line can still be found near Chirk and Dolywern. Also, above Glyn Ceiriog, part of what was the track is now used as a public footpath. The bridges still exist at Chirk, Dolywern and Pandy, former buildings can be found such as the waiting rooms at Dolywern and a locomotive shed and station at Glyn as well as some other buildings, or remnants of them, at Hendre. It is understood that the Talyllyn Railway at Tywyn (*see entry 26*) retains two restored coaches from the tramway,

On 20th July, 2010 an Arriva service from Wrexham to Chester passes through countryside near to the village of Pulford. Gresford stands on the hill in the background.   *Author*

Grade II-listed Chester station as photographed on 11th February, 2010; it is one of only 22 stations in the UK so listed. Chester station at one time was shared by the Chester & Holyhead Railway, the Chester & Crewe Railway and the Birkenhead Railway. The joint station dates from 1848 and was designed by Francis Thompson with an Italianate frontage. The station was innovative in having carved wooden owls on the roof beams to help deter pigeons! Examples can be seen clearly above platform 4.   *Author*

albeit in a modified form, and in the Narrow Gauge Railway Museum, also at Tywyn, there is nameplate from a former local locomotive.

The Project: The strategic vision of the Glyn Valley Trust is: 'To conserve and interpret the remaining features of the original Glyn Valley Tramway. To recreate an operational section of the original Glyn Valley Tramway, with sympathetic and complementary visitor facilities, to provide an attraction which will support the economy of Chirk and the Ceiriog Valley. To promote the recording, conservation and interpretation of the Economic, Social, Natural and Industrial History of the area'. There are a number of ambitious plans including the establishment of a new Visitor Centre at Chirk in conjunction with the local authorities which will embrace not only the tramway but the Llangollen Canal World Heritage Site and the Ceiriog Valley. It is also hoped to reinstate sections of working tramway, understandably in phases, i.e. beginning with a five-eighths of a mile of track operating initially with locomotives hired in especially for the occasion. There is also an interesting idea of constructing a modern-operating brick-built station on the platform at Chirk station but in a replica style. Whilst these plans and more may seem ambitious at this time, one has only to look at what has been achieved on the Ffestiniog and the Welsh Highland railways and many others to realise that all things are possible given the enthusiasm and energies of dedicated volunteers.

Neighbouring railways: Llangollen Railway and Cambrian Heritage Railways.

3 Borderlands Railway - Wrexham to Chester

Locations: Wrexham and Chester.
GPS: Wrexham: 53°2'48.87"N   2°59'30.02"W.   Chester: 53°11'32.01"N 2°53'31.58"W.
OS map references: Wrexham SJ333499. Chester: SJ404666.
Operator: Arriva Trains Wales.
Timetable: Arriva No. 4.
Route: Wrexham to Chester with no intermediate stops but passing through the villages of Gresford and Rossett.
Journey time: 18 minutes.
Websites: www.arrivatrainswales.co.uk
Operating dates: Daily all year round with services every two hours.
Railway constructions of interest: Grosvenor railway bridge over the River Dee alongside the Chester's Roodee racecourse. Chester railway station, built in 1848, was previously known as Chester General. Incidentally, in May 1972 an evening freight train hauled by a class '24' diesel locomotive and comprising 38 wagons, five of which were carrying kerosene, petrol and gas oil, suffered brake failure and ran on into a stationary diesel-multiple-unit (dmu). Fortunately the dmu was empty and few people were on the platform. The driver jumped clear on to the platform before his locomotive ploughed into the dmu completely destroying the first coach and tearing the second off its bogies and throwing it onto the platform where it destroyed the refreshment room wall. A major fire broke out when the fuel tanks burst and

An Arriva train crossing Chester's railway bridge as seen from the Grosvenor road bridge looking across the expanse of the Roodee racecourse on 11th February, 2010. Horse racing on the Roodee has gone on since 1539 but before this the site was home to the famous and bloody Goteddsday (Shrove Tuesday) football match. Due to its violent nature the match was eventually banned by the city authorities in 1533. *Author*

The memorial in All Saints' Church, Gresford to the miners who died in the Gresford mining disaster. Each day a page is turned in the book recording those who lost their lives and who are still buried hundreds of feet below ground. *Author*

ignited. The local fire brigade who were based nearby were quickly in attendance. They were able to rescue a trapped postal worker and evacuate another train before it was engulfed in flames. Fortuitously, nobody was killed and only two persons injured.

What to see locally: The ancient walled city of Chester steeped in history is a must to visit. The Welsh, though, have to take particular care when visiting Chester. Following the Battle of Shrewsbury in 1403, a Royal Proclamation was issued by Prince Henry, Earl of Chester and later King Henry V, 'all manner of Welsh persons or Welsh sympathies should be expelled from the City; that no Welshman should enter the City before sunrise or tarry in it after sunset, under pain of decapitation'. The proclamation has never been repealed!

What to remember locally: At Gresford, north of Wrexham, was the fourth worst disaster in British coal mining history. At 0200 hours on Saturday 22nd September, 1934, during the night shift at Gresford Colliery, an explosion rocked the Dennis Section of the mine. Miraculously six miners managed to scramble to safety through a return airway. Over the following weekend, rescue teams attempted to rescue any possible survivors. It was a very dangerous occupation; indeed, three rescuers were killed attempting to explore another return airway. There were no other survivors and on the evening of Sunday 23rd a decision was made to seal the mine. A total of 266 died in the disaster, all but four of whom remain entombed in the mine. It was not until 1982 that a memorial in the form of a mural was placed in All Saints' Church to remember the lost miners. On a table nearby there is a book of remembrance, a page of the names of the lost being turned each day. For the record, the worst coal mining disaster in British mining history was also in Wales at Senghenydd near Caerphilly in 1913 when 439 men and boys lost their lives.

What to hear locally: The peal of bells in the medieval Church of All Saints' at Gresford is one of the Seven Wonders of Wales.

Neighbouring railways: Llangollen Railway. North Wales Coast line operates from Chester to Holyhead on Anglesey.

4 Borderlands Railway - Wrexham to Bidston (Merseyside)

Locations: Wrexham and Bidston.
GPS: Wrexham: 53°2'48.87"N 2°59'30.02"W. Bidston: 53°24'15.55"N 3°3'56.30"W.
OS map reference: Wrexham: SJ333499 Bidston: SJ285905.
Operator: Arriva Trains Wales.
Timetable: Arriva No. 4.
Route: Wrexham for Bidston on Merseyside's Wirral Peninsular, England via Gwersyllt, Cefn-y-bedd, Caergwrle, Hope, Rhos-y-brwyher (Penffordd), Little Mountain, Hawarden, Shotton, Hawarden Bridge and into England over the River Dee with the first station located at Neston.
Journey time: 32 minutes.
Websites: www.arrivatrainswales.co.uk
Operating dates: Daily every hour.

The Hawarden Bridge was built in 1889 to cross the River Dee at Shotton, as seen here on 10th August 2009.   *Author*

Railway constructions of interest: The Hawarden Railway Bridge over the River Dee, near Shotton was built as part of the Chester & Connah's Quay Railway. Opening in 1889, the central section used to be a swing bridge but is now welded together but the rotating mechanism can still be seen.

Whom to have known locally: Hawarden's most famous residents include the 19th century Prime Minister, William Ewart Gladstone (1809-1898), who lived in Hawarden Castle which was the seat of his wife's family, the Glynnes. Gladstone bequeathed his library, now known as the St Deiniol's Library, to the town. His descendants continue to live in Hawarden with the current incumbent being Sir William Gladstone who is the Lord Lieutenant of Clwyd. Emma, Lady Hamilton (1761-1815) who is perhaps best remembered as the mistress of Lord Horatio Nelson was brought up by her mother at Hawarden. She was born 'Amy Lyon' in Neston on the Wirral which was then in Cheshire, the daughter of a local blacksmith who died when she was only two years old. Although she had no formal education, she first pursued a career on the stage through which she met the rich and famous. In 1791, she married Sir William Hamilton. In Naples two years later, as a guest and close friend of Queen Maria Carolina, the wife of Ferdinand I of Naples, she met Nelson for the first time. Nelson returned to Naples in 1798; his adventures had already taken a toll on him - he had lost an arm and most of his teeth and was given to fits of coughing. Lady Hamilton, forever the actress, reportedly threw herself upon him in admiration, calling out, 'Oh God, is it possible?' as she fainted against him! Another currently well-known resident is the professional footballer Michael Owen (b. 1979) who, although born a few miles away in Chester and therefore eligible to play for the England football team, was raised in Hawarden and at one time lived a few miles away at Northop. In the nearby village of Ewloe Owen famously bought a small street of houses for his extended family.

What to see locally: At Parkgate near Neston on the Wirral is the RSPB's Gayton Sands reserve where large flocks of wading birds gather on the salt marsh. Near to Corus-owned Shotton steelworks is the spectacular Flintshire bridge spanning the River Dee which was built between 1994 and 1997 at a cost of £55 million.

Neighbouring railways: Llangollen Railway, North Wales Coast Line from Chester to Holyhead on Anglesey.

5 North Wales Coast Line - Chester to Llandudno Junction

Locations: Chester and Llandudno Junction.
GPS: Chester: 53°11′29.25″N 2°53′42.03″W. Llandudno Junction: 53°17′9.87″N 3°48′38.59″W.
OS map references: Chester: SJ404666 Llandudno Junction: SH798779.
Operator: Arriva Trains Wales and Virgin Trains.
Timetable: Arriva No. 4 and Virgin D.
Route: Chester to Llandudno Junction via Shotton, Flint, Prestatyn, Rhyl, Abergele & Pensarn and Colwyn Bay, a distance of 52 miles.
Journey time: About one hour on Arriva Trains and 53 minutes by Virgin Trains.
Websites: www.arrivatrainswales.co.uk and www.virgintrains.com
Operating dates: Daily with reduced services on Saturdays and Sundays.
What to see locally: The coastal resorts of Prestatyn, Rhyl, Colwyn Bay and Llandudno are all worthy of visits especially for those with young children to entertain. A visit to the oldest continuously-operating pilgrimage site of St Winefride's Well (sometimes spelled St Winifred) at Holywell in Flintshire is most interesting as is the legend surrounding it. It is said that it was in the 7th century that a young prince named Caradoc visited Tegeingle near the mouth of the River Dee. Caradoc saw a pretty young girl called Winefride and made advances towards her which she rejected. She ran away towards the church. Caradoc, furious at being spurned, chased after her. When he caught up with her, he killed her by cutting off her head with his sword. The head rolled down the hill towards the church. Winefride's father, (later St) Beuno, was just leaving the church and realizing what had happened cursed Caradoc who is said to have immediately fallen dead. Beuno lifted her head, wrapped it in his cloak and returned to the church, where he asked the congregation to help him pray for Winefride. It is said that he then joined her 'head to her body and she at once revived, and afterwards bearing only a red threadlike mark around her throat'. There are various versions of this story. Holywell is described as the 'Lourdes' of Wales. Records exist going back to the 12th century describing the cures claimed after bathing in the waters. There is a splendid collection of wooden crutches discarded by those who have benefited!
Neighbouring railways: Great Orme Tramway from Llandudno Victoria station. Conwy Valley Railway (North) and (South).

'The North Wales Coast Express' hauled by steam locomotive LMS 'Princess Coronation' class No. 6233 *Duchess of Sutherland* heading for its ultimate destination, Holyhead, on 2nd August 2009 on an excursion organized by the Railway Touring Company.   *Autho*

An Arriva class '175' approaches Colwyn Bay on 5th August, 2009. The busy A55 - the North Wales Expressway - from Chester to Bangor runs alongside.   *Author*

Virgin Voyager No. 221.117 photographed at Bagillt in Flintshire on 20th July, 2009. The sands of Holywell Bank stretching over to the Hilbre and Middle Eye islands (*to the right on the horizon*) provide the background to this train speeding towards Chester. The islands are a well-known bird sanctuary as well as home to the rare natterjack toad.   *Author*

The rare USA-built 4-4-0 Cagney No. 44, built *circa* 1910, hauls its train around the Marine Lake at Rhyl on 18th April, 2010.   *Author*

6 Rhyl Miniature Railway

Location: Rhyl, Denbighshire.
GPS: Rhyl: 53°18′34.07″N 3°31′49.55″W
OS map references: Rhyl: SJ008811. Rhyl Marine Lake: SH999806
Operator: Rhyl Steam Preservation Trust.
Contact details: Rhyl Steam Preservation Trust, 10, Cilnant, Mold, Flintshire CH7 1GG.
Route: The Marine Lake at Rhyl, a distance of one mile.
Gauge: 15 in.
Traction: The railway operates four 4-4-2 Albert Barnes & Co. steam locomotives: Nos. 101 *Joan* (1920), 102 *Railway Queen* (1921), 105 *Michael* (*circa* 1925) and 105 *Billy* (*circa* 1930). In addition there is a rare USA-built 4-4-0 Cagney (*circa* 1910), *Clara* a Guest & Saunders Light Engineering S/O 0-4-2 DN (1961) a Hayne/Minirail 2W-2-4 BER (1983) and a 4wDM Lister (1938). There is an interesting collection of carriages some almost 100 years old. Included are two Cagneys; one, very rare, believed to be over 100 years old and the second, a replica using original Cagney ironwork, which was originally made in Lima, Peru. Steam trains operate on peak days and every Sunday and also during the summer holidays on Thursdays and Saturdays. Other times rides are in the electric railcar or on diesel-hauled trains.
Website: www.rhylminiaturerailway.co.uk/
Operating dates: Weekends from early April to late September, Bank Holiday Mondays, and daily from mid-July to late August. Trains normally run from 1100 to 1600 hours. Santa Specials run on the two Sundays before Christmas.
History: The railway first opened on 1st May, 1911 and is Britain's oldest miniature line. The railway was originally designed by Henry Greenly who thought that the Marine Lake was an ideal place for a miniature line. As the popularity of UK-based holidays declined in the late 1970s the railway suffered economically. In 1980, a local businessman Mr Les Hughes came to the rescue and by becoming the owner of most of the railway's locomotives and carriages he allowed the railway to stay in steam. In 2001, Rhyl Steam Preservation Trust, of which Mr Hughes is the Chairman, took over the running of the railway. In March 2006, a new station building and a museum were built with funding from the Heritage Lottery Fund, Denbighshire EC Key Fund, the Welsh Assembly Government and Rhyl Town Council. For a comprehensive account of the history of the railway visit the website.
What to see locally: One of the UK's smallest ancient cathedrals, built in the 13th century, can be visited at St Asaph. St Kentigern built his church here in AD 560 and 13 years later he left Asaph as his successor. Since then the cathedral and diocese has been dedicated to St Asaph. In the same diocese at Bodelwyddan is the beautiful white 'Marble Church' dedicated to St Margaret, an outstanding local landmark running alongside the A55 road. The building in fact is constructed of limestone but obtains its name from the 13 types of marble decorating the interior.
Whom to remember locally: The Rt Hon. John Prescott MP, former Deputy Prime Minister, was born at nearby Prestatyn. Rhyl was the scene of a notorious event in the 2001 election campaign when a farmer threw an egg at him.

Prescott, a former amateur boxer, responded immediately by hitting the man directly on the jaw; neither man was prosecuted. Ruth Ellis, the last woman to be executed in the United Kingdom, was born in Rhyl in 1926.

Neighbouring railways: North Wales Coast line from Chester to Llandudno Junction.

Comments: There is a museum and a shop. An active *Friends of Rhyl Miniature Railway* supports the Rhyl Steam Preservation Trust.

7 North Wales Coast Line - Llandudno Junction to Bangor

Locations: Llandudno Junction and Bangor.
GPS: Llandudno Junction: 53°17′9.87″N 3°48′38.59″W. Bangor: 53°13′40.06″N 4°8′2.43″W.
OS map references: Llandudno Junction: SH798779 Bangor: SH575715.
Operator: Arriva Trains Wales and Virgin Trains.
Timetables: Arriva No. 4 and Virgin D.
Route: Llandudno Junction to Bangor via Conwy, Penmaenmawr and Llanfairfechan, a distance of 17 miles.
Journey time: About 21 minutes by both Arriva Trains Wales and Virgin Trains.
Websites: www.arrivatrainwales.co.uk   www.virgintrains.co.uk
Operating dates: Daily frequent services but reduced services on Saturdays and Sundays.
Railway constructions of interest: Conwy Castle railway bridge is a wrought-iron tubular bridge built by Robert Stephenson in 1848 and, following the disastrous Britannia Bridge fire in the Menai, it is now the only surviving example of this style undertaken by him. Apart from extra columns reinforcing the bridge it is otherwise unchanged since it was opened in 1849.

An Arriva service passes on the river side of Conwy Castle on 16th February, 2009. The railway bridge's architecture (*seen to the right*) has been tastefully blended in with the castle's original fortifications.   *Author*

What to remember locally: On 27th August, 1950 six people were killed in the sleeping compartment of the 'Irish Mail' train from Holyhead. The accident occurred near Penmaenmawr and was caused by signalman error when a slow train had been allowed onto the track into the path of the speeding express. It was estimated that the speed of the mail train was 70 mph when the impact occurred.

What to see locally: The coastal resort of Llandudno is Wales's largest holiday resort, uniquely situated between two hills, the Great Orme and the Little Orme. It has two marvellous beaches, the award winning North Shore and the quieter, sand-duned West Shore. Nearby Conwy is a World Heritage Site of Significant European Importance. It has numerous historic buildings including a 14th century merchant's house, a magnificent Elizabethan town house and what is believed to be the smallest house in Great Britain, all this in addition to a picturesque and busy harbour. Conwy Castle, built between 1283 and 1289 by King Edward I, dominates the estuary with vast panoramic views looking towards the mountains of Snowdonia. The RSPB's Conwy Nature Reserve is a haven for wading birds and wildfowl and is easily accessed from the main A55 road near to Llandudno Junction.

Neighbouring railways: The Great Orme Tramway from Llandudno Victoria station. Located at Llanberis, 12 miles from Bangor is the Snowdon Mountain Railway and the Llanberis Lake Railway. The narrow gauge Welsh Mountain Railway operates from Caernarfon nine miles from Bangor.

8 North Wales Coast Line - Bangor to Holyhead on the Island of Anglesey

Locations: Bangor, Gwynedd and Holyhead on Anglesey.
GPS: Bangor: 53°13'40.06"N 4°8'2.43"W. Holyhead: 53°18'27.48"N 4°37'52.46"W.
OS map references: Bangor: SH575715 Holyhead: SH249824.
Operator: Arriva Trains Wales and Virgin Trains (Super Voyager).
Route: Bangor to Holyhead on the Island of Anglesey via Llanfairpwllgwyngyll (Llanfair PG), Bodorgan, Ty Croes, Rhosneigr, and Valley, a distance of about 34 miles.
Journey time: About 40 minutes with Arriva Trains Wales and 30 minutes by Virgin Trains.
Websites: www.arrivatrainswales.co.uk www.virgintrains.com
Operating dates: Daily with reduced services on Saturdays and Sundays.
Railway constructions of interest: Of particular interest is the Britannia Bridge (w. *Pont Britannia*) which crosses the Menai Strait from the mainland on to the Island of Anglesey (w. *Ynys Môn*). The original construction, a tubular bridge of wrought iron rectangular box-section spans, was built by Robert Stephenson (son of locomotive engineer George Stephenson) and opened in 1850. The original bridge operated without problems for 120 years. Unfortunately, during an evening in May 1970 the bridge was severely damaged when boys playing there started a fire. The damage caused by the fire was very severe, indeed only the limestone pillars remained. The bridge had to be completely rebuilt as a

The Britannia railway and road bridge as taken from St Tysilio's church on Church Island in the Menai Strait on 24th July, 2009. The white building is on Ynys Gorad Goch (e. the island of the red weirs). The island is situated between the Menai suspension bridge and Britannia bridge has another name 'fish trap island' which provides a better clue as to the purpose of the walls around the island. The walls form weirs or gorads that trap fish on the eddying tide. Herring was a popular catch and these, when caught, were smoked on the island. The fishing business has long since gone but the house is still occupied. The Virgin train can just about be seen on the right of the bridge at the lower level.   *Author*

The shopping emporium adjoining the local railway station at Llanfair PG.   *Author*

The 1880-built curved Holyhead station with Arriva's dmu No. 175101 leaving for Bangor on 24th July, 2009.   *Author*

steel box girder bridge with its deck supported by archways. It has two levels; the lower carries the railway line and the upper a single-carriageway section of the A55 trunk road. Incidentally Stephenson's only other tubular iron railway bridge crosses the River Conwy near Llandudno Junction; it was built two years before his Britannia Bridge and fortunately remains intact. Also worth seeing is the long curved railway station at Holyhead, construction of which began in 1875 by the London & North Western Railway (LNWR) and was formally opened by HRH The Prince of Wales in 1880. A magnificent Whitchurch clock housed in a tower outside the modern Stena Lines offices commemorates this event.

What to know locally: After passing over the Britannia Bridge and on to the Isle of Anglesey the first station is at Lllanfairpwllgwyngyllgogerychwyrndrobwl-lllantysiliogogogochuchaf which translates to mean 'The church of St Mary in the hollow of white hazel trees near the rapid whirlpool by St Tysilio's of the red cave'. (NB: The local shop emporium presents a slightly different translation!) Originally the village was called up until the mid-19th century, Llanfairpwllgwyngyll, more often shortened by the locals to Llanfair PG. It is said that the village changed the name on the suggestion of a local cobbler from Menai Bridge in order to encourage local tourism. Judging by the number of persons who stop to photograph the village/station/shop signs, the initiative has proved to be a continuing success. The first ever meeting of the Women's Institute took place in Llanfair PG in 1915. The movement, which had first begun in Canada, then spread rapidly to the rest of Great Britain.

The station building at Llanfair PG.   *Author*

What to see locally: The Menai suspension bridge built by Thomas Telford in 1826 can be found further up the Menai Strait from the Britannia Bridge towards Bangor. The Menai Strait is not easy water for mariners and certainly not for swimmers. The cause is the differential tides at each end of the 14-mile stretch of water. The most dangerous area is between the two bridges and is known as the Swellies (w. *Pwll Ceris*). The rocks here near the surface cause over-falls and local whirlpools, which can be of considerable danger in themselves and can cause small boats to founder on the rocks. This was in fact what happened to the school ship HMS *Conway* which foundered here in April 1953. It remained on the rocks for three years before it caught fire in unexplained circumstances and burned down to the waterline. For those interested in bird-watching perhaps one of the best sites to observe a variety of birds in north-west Wales is at the RSPB reserve on the cliffs at South Stack on the western side of the Island of Anglesey. As well as various gulls particular species include the puffin, guillemot, razorbill and the chough. If one observes a flurry of activity whilst watching the local bird population it probably will have been caused by a peregrine falcon. The ferry port at Holyhead is interesting to watch as ships come and go.

Neighbouring railways: Arriva and Virgin Trains cross the Britannia Bridge. Not far away can be found the Welsh Highland Railway, the Welsh Highland Heritage Railway, the Snowdon Mountain Railway and the Llanberis Lake railway.

9 Conwy Valley (North) - Llandudno Junction to Llandudno (Town station)

Locations: Llandudno Junction and Llandudno Town station, Augusta Street, LL30 2AF.
GPS: Llandudno Junction: 53°17'9.87"N 3°48'38.59"W. Llandudno Town Station: 53°19'15.24"N 3°49'37.34"W.
OS map references: Llandudno Junction: SH798779. Llandudno Town: SH783819.
Operator: Arriva Trains Wales.
Timetable number: Arriva Trains Wales No. 4.
Route: Llandudno Junction to Llandudno station in the town via Deganwy, location of the former docks.
Journey time: 10 minutes.
Website: www.arrivatrainswales.co.uk
Operating dates: Daily with reduced services on Saturdays and Sundays.
Railway constructions of interest: Stephenson's Conwy railway bridge.
What to see locally: The coastal holiday resort of Llandudno is probably the most popular in the whole of Wales. Nearby Deganwy is a delightful small resort which captures some of the finest views of Snowdonia, the Conwy river, its estuary and the castle. Further afield across the Conwy Bay there are views of Puffin Island and Anglesey. Deganwy was also a port and from the late 19th century slate was transported by rail from Blaenau Ffestiniog to the quayside and then transferred to sailing ships for export abroad. Conwy Castle was built between 1283 and 1289 by Edward I and dominates the estuary and river. On a hillock above Deganwy, known as the Faerdre, are the ruins of the original

An Arriva train passing between the two courses of Llandudno Golf Club and North Wales Golf Club on 22nd July, 2009.   *Author*

No. 4 tram leaves Llandudno on its way up to the summit of the Great Orme on 22nd July, 2009.
Caroline Jones

castle destroyed by Prince Llywelyn ab Iorwerth (e. the Great) in 1263. Incidentally, there is a statue in Conwy town square dedicated to Llywelyn ab Iorwerth. The first castle was built on this site in 1070 by the Norman Baron Robert of Rhuddlan.

Neighbouring railways: Great Orme Tramway from Llandudno Victoria station to the summit of Great Orme.

10 Great Orme Tramway

Location: Llandudno Victoria station, Church Walks, LL30 2NB.

GPS: Victoria station: 53°19′20.80″N 3°49′36.91″W.

OS map references: Llandudno Victoria Station: SH777827. Great Orme Station: SH766833.

Operator: Conwy County Borough Council - Great Orme Tramway.

Contact details: Great Orme Tramway, Victoria Station, Church Walks, Llandudno. LL30 2NB. Telephone: 01492 879306. E-mail: tramwayenquiries@conwy.gov.uk

Route: Llandudno Victoria station to the Great Orme summit at 679 ft (207 m.) via Halfway station.

Journey time: 15 minutes.

Distance: One mile.

Website: www.greatormetramway.co.uk

Operating dates: Daily from late March to late October with services every 20 minutes between 1000 and 1800 hours, but ending an hour earlier in March and October.

Halfway station where there is an interesting exhibition about the tramway and its history. *Author*

On 22nd July, 2009 Arriva's dmu No. 150282 leaves the small station which serves the community of Llansanffraid Glan Conwy heading ultimately for Blaenau Ffestiniog.   *Author*

Southbound, near Llansanffraid Glan Conwy, is an Arriva service passing by the river on a flood tide on 22nd July, 2009, observed by that Jack Russell terrier again!   *Author*

History: During the Victorian era, roads on the Great Orme were primitive which with steep slopes denied many from reaching the summit and enjoying the panoramic views. Towards the end of the 19th century Llandudno had become increasingly popular as a tourist resort which provoked a group of local businessmen to build a tramway to the summit. It took a little over 15 months to construct. On completion it was declared safe by the Board of Trade and on 31st July, 1902 the first tram departed from Victoria station, to the accompaniment of the local town band playing 'God Save the King'.

Railway constructions of interest: Halfway station.

What to see and remember locally: At the top of the Great Orme a nine-bedroom hotel was built in the early part of the 20th century. Given the Great Orme's strategic location it was requisitioned by the Royal Air Force in 1941 and became a radar station. After the war the hotel was returned to civilian status and in 1952 Randolph Aldolphus Turpin, the famous champion middleweight boxer, became the resident licensee. However the business began to fail as Turpin experienced financial difficulties with the Inland Revenue. Eventually Llandudno Urban Council bought him out in 1961. He returned to boxing for a short while but was forced to retire with troubled eyesight. He took his own life in 1966 at the age of 37. The former hotel is now called the Summit Complex and is very popular with visitors especially those interested in the sport of boxing. Randolph Turpin memorabilia is abundant in the bar, the themed restaurant, the cafeteria and the gift shop. A cable car offering spectacular views of the North Wales coast also operates to the summit in the holiday season. TV presenter Paula Yates (1960-2000) was born in nearby Colwyn Bay; she was married to singer, and figurehead of Band Aid and Live Aid Bob Geldof.

Neighbouring railways: Arriva trains travel to Llandudno station from Llandudno Junction.

11
Conwy Valley (South) - Llandudno Junction to Blaenau Ffestiniog

Locations: Llandudno Junction and Blaenau Ffestiniog.

GPS: Llandudno Junction: 53°17'9.87"N 3°48'38.59"W. Blaenau Ffestiniog: 52°59'18.37"N 3°55'38.90"W.

OS map references: Llandudno Junction: SH798779. Blaenau Ffestiniog: SH695463.

Operator: Arriva Trains Wales.

Timetable number: Arriva Trains Wales No. 4.

Route: Llandudno Junction to Blaenau Ffestiniog via Glan Conwy, Tal-y-Cafn, Dolgarrog, Gogledd/North Llanrwst, Llanrwst, Betws-y-Coed, Pont-y-Pant, Dolwyddelan and Roman Bridge, a distance of 28 miles.

Journey time: 1 hour.

Website: www.arrivatrainswales.co.uk

Operating dates: Daily about every three hours.

History: The first section of this railway from Llandudno Junction to Llanrwst (north) was concluded in 1863. Five years later its extension to Betws-y-Coed was completed. With the growth of the slate industry around Blaenau Ffestiniog

Tal-y-Cafn station on 8th March, 2010. The level crossing is still manually operated and is one of the few railway platforms in Wales which are mown in summer! *Author*

A late morning Arriva service crossing Pont Gethin on its way to Blaenau Ffestiniog on 8th March, 2010. *Author*

the railway was extended to there by 1879. The railway was critical to the transportation of slate and other mined material to the docks at Deganwy but passengers were also carried. Between the late 19th century and up to the mid-20th century the line transported considerable volumes of freight traffic. However, with the development of modern roofing materials, the authentic slate business diminished so that by 1984 all freight traffic had ended. The line is now used by commuters to Llandudno and is also a popular tourist facility. The route, much of which is single-track, climbs through spectacular mountain scenery attaining an altitude of 790 ft (243 m.). At this point trains enter the tunnel under Moel Dyrnogydd on the run down to the station at Blaenau Ffestiniog. The station here is shared with the narrow gauge Ffestiniog Railway.

Railway constructions of interest: The up platform at Tal-y-Cafn station has been the subject of a refurbishment project carried out by volunteers from the Llandudno & Conwy Valley Railway Society; note the hand-made replica of the station running-in board reflecting the LNWR era which is the main feature on the platform.

Pont Gethin (GPS: 53°4'1.23" 3°49'15.02") is a railway viaduct over the A470 which carries trains through the Lledr valley to and from Blaenau Ffestiniog. It was built in 1879 by Owen Gethin Jones and is now a listed building. Before trains arrive at Blaenau Ffestiniog the line passes through the Moel Dyrnogydd tunnel, built by the engineer (not the bookseller!) W.H. Smith in 1879. It is two and a half miles long making it the longest single-track tunnel in the United Kingdom.

What to see locally: At Tal-y-Cafn the line passes close to the site of a Roman encampment, Caerhun, where also stands the beautiful Church of St Mary built in the 13th century. The bridge at Tal-y-Cafn was constructed in 1897 to replace a ferry service; it is the first crossing of the river since the Conwy town bridge. Further along is the Dolgarrog halt from where it is ideal to take a walk across the river on the girder bridge which served the former rail line to the local aluminium works (*see next entry*). Above the village of Dolgarrog the heavily-wooded slopes of Coed Dolgarrog rise and to the left are the dramatic cliffs of Clogwyn Mawr. High above the valley is the site of the medieval township of Ardda and the spectacular waterfalls of the Afon Ddu. Later, two miles after Betws-y-Coed, the railway passes close to the Swallow Falls (w. *Rhaeadr Ewynnol*). The waterfall on the Afon Llugwy has been popular with tourists for over a hundred years. The main viewpoints are on the southern bank of the river but more dramatic views can be seen by approaching on foot on the northern bank. Earlier on the route is Llanrwst which, on visiting today, it is surprising to learn that at one time it was the eighth largest town in Wales even bigger than Cardiff! A feature in the town is the narrow three-arch stone bridge, *Pont Fawr*, said to have been designed by Inigo Jones and built in 1636 by the baronet Sir John Wynn who at that time lived in the exquisite fortified manor house, Gwydir Castle. The castle has the reputation for being one of the most haunted houses in Wales. Many local people will testify to having seen ghosts in the castle, the 'Grey Lady' being the most commonly seen, together with the ghost of a monk said to have been trapped in a tunnel leading from a secret room. The property is now in private ownership.

LMS Stanier class '5' No. 45231 *Sherwood Forester* on a steam excursion emerges from the tunnel under Moel Dyrnogydd on its final approach to Blaenau Ffestiniog on 5th August, 2009. The Railway Touring Company organized the trip as 'The Welsh Mountaineer'. *Author*

Whom to have known locally: Professor Gwyn Thomas was born in 1936 in Tanygrisiau, near to Blaenau Ffestiniog. He is a Welsh poet and at one time was the National Poet for Wales. In 1979 he was commissioned to write a short poem to celebrate the opening of *Hafod Eryri*, the then new summit building at the top of Snowdon:

> *The summit of Snowdon, here you are nearer to heaven*
> *The rocks record the aeons of creation*
> *It's our duty to guard this glory*
> *Here you will see tempests and tranquillity*
> *All around us are the grandeur and the anguish of an old, old nation*

Neighbouring railways: This Arriva route connects with the Ffestiniog Railway at Blaenau Ffestiniog station.

Arriva service approaches Blaenau Ffestiniog on 8th March, 2010.   *Author*

12 Dolgarrog Railway Society

Location: Dolgarrog.
GPS: Dolgarrog: 53°11′7.16″N 3°50′26.19″W.
OS map reference: Dolgarrog: SH769669.
Operator: Dolgarrog Railway Society Ltd.
Contact details: Dolgarrog Railway Society Limited, 'Llanerch', 2, Pwll y Waen, Ty'n y Groes, Conwy, LL32 8TQ.
Project: The aims of the Dolgarrog Railway Society are to re-establish a small industrial railway line at Dolgarrog and to preserve locomotives and rolling stock which could have been found on the line. The society was formed about 10 years ago and first established a base at Tal-y-Cafn about three miles north of Dolgarrog; from there plans were laid for the construction of a heritage railway in the Conwy Valley. From early on the society purchased and restored several items of rolling stock as well as a small diesel shunting locomotive, together with various items of railwayana. Later, Dolgarrog Aluminium Limited generously granted a lease for use of the trackbed of the old Dolgarrog Railway which originally served the aluminium works. The project proposal is to lay track over much of the old trackbed and to build a depot at the works end of the line. A timescale as yet has not been announced.
Gauge: Standard.
Traction & rolling stock: The society owns an 0-4-0 diesel-mechanical locomotive *Taurus* built in 1951 by the Vulcan Foundry, a BR standard 20 ton goods brake van, a BR standard 12 ton ventilated goods van and BR 13 ton pipe wagon. Members are now on the look-out for a five-plank wagon and more trackwork for the route.

The former railway bridge over the River Conwy near Dolgarrog as seen on 8th March, 2010. *Author*

Website: www.dolgarrograilway.co.uk
Operating dates: Yet to be determined.
History of the Dolgarrog Works: With the promise of cheap electricity. generated by water flowing from the reservoir high above the village of Dolgarrog, plans were drawn up in 1907 to build an aluminium works and the following year production began. Unfortunately for the company there was a downturn in the price of aluminium quickly forcing the enterprise into liquidation. Happily, not least for the local workforce, a second company was established in 1909. Transport of material to and from the works was a problem from the outset for the main road and the Conwy Valley Railway (Llandudno Junction to Blaenau Ffestiniog) operated by the LNWR were on the 'wrong' side of the river. Initially, the company took advantage of the river and employed steam vessels, for example, a 40 ton steam boat, the *Pioneer*, and unpowered barges to transport material to a former Russian whaling ship, the *Anna Olga*, which was used as a floating warehouse in Conwy Harbour. A 2 ft gauge tramway was built to make the connection from the works to the landing stage on the river. However, it was not long before the company established a connection via a girder bridge to the LNWR main line. Initially used for freight transport the company soon decided to run passenger services for the benefit of its employees, some of whom would arrive by the main line services. Passenger services were operated for a number of years but were withdrawn about 1932. Freight continued, reaching its peak during World War II. However, a decline began in the 1950s and by 1960 the line was scarcely used leading to its inevitable closure with the track being lifted a few years later. One section of track is still visible today not far from the works in Station Road. The trackbed to the bridge can still be found but, as one might guess, nature has played its part over five decades with much of it now being overgrown by trees. For an interesting and detailed account of this former railway and the locomotives which served it, see the history pages on the society's website.
Railway constructions of interest: The girder bridge over the River Conwy still exists but is now used as a footpath and to carry piped mains water.
What to remember locally: The Dolgarrog Disaster occurred in the 1920s when floodwaters breached the Eigiau dam and caused a hamlet and a village to be swept away. On Monday 2nd November, 1925, after a fortnight of heavy rain, a breach in a small gravity dam occurred at the Aluminium Corporation's Llyn Eigiau reservoir, up in the hills near Craig Eigiau (alt. 735 m.). At the time the breach was said to have been caused by inadequate foundations and lack of maintenance. The breach released thousands of gallons of water which flowed down the Porth Llwyd river and into another small reservoir, the Coedty. This reservoir could not contain the extra water. As a consequence, it was also breached releasing an even greater quantity of water carrying huge boulders and sections of pipeline down the mountain through the hamlet of Porth Llwyd and onto the village of Dolgarrog, a further mile downstream. Houses were swept away and villagers with them; in all, 16 people tragically died.
Neighbouring railways: Conwy Valley Railway Museum at Betwys-y-Coed and the Conwy Valley (South) line from Llandudno Junction to Blaenau Ffestiniog.

13 Conwy Valley Railway Museum

Location: Betws-y-Coed.
GPS: Betws-y-Coed: 53°5'37.57"N 3°48'22.87"W.
OS map reference: Betws-y-Coed: SH796569.
Operator: Conwy Valley Railway Museum.
Contact details: Conwy Valley Railway Museum, The Old Goods Yard, Betws-y-Coed
LL24 0AL. Telephone: 01690 710568. E-mail@ info@www.conwyrailmuseum.co.uk
Website: www.conwyrailmuseum.co.uk
Operating dates: Daily from 1000 to 1700 hours except for the Christmas break.
The last entry is 30 minutes before closing time. Trains operate from 1015 to
1630 hours on most days.
Of interest: See the quarter full size steam locomotive 'Britannia' in the
museum - it is accurate in every detail and presented in immaculate condition.
Ride on the narrow gauge electric tramcar for over half a mile and also on one
of the steam trains (subject to weather conditions and availability) on an eight-
minute journey over a distance of one mile through lovely garden scenery. The
Denver and Rio Grande 'C19' is also an absolute delight to see steaming. The
museum contains an interesting exposition of signalling systems, train layouts
and other working models. The shop is extremely well stocked with railway
models of most gauges including original LGB locomotives and rolling stock
which are now difficult to find.

The Conwy Valley Railway Museum's diesel locomotive *Gwydir* passes the main line
station at Betws-y-Coed on 8th March, 2010.   *Author*

Gwydir makes a tour of the route before taking the first passengers of the day on 8th March, 2010.

Author

The Conwy Valley Railway Museum's steam locomotive *Douglas* had a day off on 8th March, 2010.

Author

What to see locally: The spectacular Swallow Falls (entry charge) are two miles from Betwys-y-Coed on the Holyhead Road towards Capel Curig. In Betws-y-Coed one can see Thomas Telford's iron Waterloo Bridge built in 1815. Carrying the A5 across the River Conwy, it bears the inscription: *This arch was constructed in the same year the Battle of Waterloo was fought.* It is interesting that it did not record the victory, or perhaps it was written by the French who dispute who won! At the very heart of the Snowdonia National Park is the mountain village of Capel Curig, a mecca for climbing and walking in Snowdonia. Encircled by the Glyders, Moel Siabod and the foothills of the Carneddau range, Capel Curig is the home of Plas-y-Brenin which is the national centre for mountain activities. Also in Capel Curig is *Ty Hyll* (e. The Ugly House) which derives its name from the huge, uneven boulders in its walls. The building is the home of the Snowdonia Society. *Neighbouring railways*: Ffestiniog Railway at Blaenau Ffestiniog and Arriva's Conway Valley Railway passes through Betws-y-Coed and the museum can be easily accessed over the footbridge from the station platform.

Comments: Refreshments are available in the café on site which is open from 1000 hours. The café and facility is available for private bookings. There is wheelchair access to the museum from the separate private car park. This is an excellent museum and miniature railway operated by most friendly staff; it is well worth a visit not only by railway enthusiasts but all the family with the convenience of arriving by car or by an Arriva regular service train.

14 Penrhyn Railway Society and Railway Heritage Trust

Location: Llandygai, near Bangor.
GPS: Llandygai: 53°13'0.23"N 4°6'5.72"W.
OS map reference: Llandygai: SH598709.
Operator: Penrhyn Railway Society and the Penrhyn Railway Heritage Trust.
E-mail: admin@penrhyn.co.uk
Gauge: 1 ft 10¾ in.
Website: www.penrhynrailway.co.uk
History of the quarry railway: Slate was first quarried at Penrhyn in about 1715 from an outcrop of rock located in the parish of Llanllechid. In 1785, Richard Pennant, later the first Lord Penrhyn, took over the local estate and quarry and pursued ambitious plans for its development. From 1790, the small riverside wharf near Bangor was extended in stages in 1796 and 1818 to become Port Penrhyn. The existing Roman road from Bangor to Bethesda was rebuilt to make it suitable for the heavier traffic. Bethesda. By 1801, a narrow gauge railway, just over six miles long, had been installed from the quarries to Port Penrhyn making it the first railway to be built for the carriage of slate. The rails were of iron attached to iron sleepers. These proved to be inadequate and the sleepers were soon replaced with slate and the rails fixed to iron chairs. The wagons at that time were hauled by horses. Penrhyn Quarry thus had an economic route to the sea which made the business an early leader in the budding Welsh slate industry. In 1876, the railway was rebuilt on a new route with steel rails laid on wooden sleepers. The first steam traction introduced was

The former Penrhyn Quarry locomotive *Blanche* is now regularly deployed on the Ffestiniog Railway. It was photographed at Porthmadog on 17th January, 2010.　　　　*Author*

The former Penrhyn Quarry locomotive *Jubilee 1897,* built by Manning, Wardle & Co. Ltd of Leeds, is now on display in the Narrow Gauge Museum at Tywyn.　　　　*Author*

with a locomotive constructed by Henry Hughes & Co. of Loughborough. A number of locomotives, built by the engineers De Winton & Co. of Caernarfon, soon followed. One of these, *George Henry*, can be seen in the Narrow Gauge Railway Museum (NGRM) at Tywyn (*see entry 27*). Between 1882 and 1909 the Hunslet Engine Company of Leeds supplied 16 four-wheeled locomotives. From 1922 onwards a further 15 locomotives were bought second-hand from various sources. *Jubilee 1897*, built by Manning, Wardle & Co. Ltd of Leeds, was one of these; it also resides in the NGRM museum. The railway was totally private, providing no public services for goods or passengers apart from a short period in the 1870s when it was also used to transport grain from the mills nearby. Quarrymen's trains did run but these were paid for by the quarrymen themselves! Declining demand for real slate, the manufacture of substitute roofing materials and the greater use of road transport led to the railway closing in 1962. All the surviving locomotives fortunately were sold off for preservation, among them *Blanche* and *Linda*, both built by Hunslet in 1893 and which can now be seen working on the Ffestiniog Railway (*see entry 18*). Other locomotives and rolling stock are to be found in the museum at Penrhyn Castle. The quarry at Penrhyn was extensively modernized between 1964 and 1967. It was owned and operated by Alfred McAlpine Slate but has subsequently been sold. It the largest company in the slate industry, each year producing over 10,000 tons of slate. (Source: NGRM.)

Preservation history: The Penrhyn Railway Heritage Trust was formed by local enthusiasts in 2004 with the aims of preserving items connected with the Penrhyn Quarry Railway and ultimately to recreate the railway or part of it. The Penrhyn Railway Society was launched in mid-2005 and has already gathered a significant membership. The society plays a vital part in the development of the project by organizing volunteer groups and raising funds without which progress would not be made. Society membership is open to all, details of which can be obtained on the website. The society produces an acclaimed quarterly journal entitled *Y Llechen* / The Slate.

Neighbouring railways: North Wales Coast line to Bangor.

What to see locally: The 19th century built neo-Norman Penrhyn Castle (GPS: 53°13'3.13"N 4°5'53.06"W) which includes an industrial railway museum. Also contained in the castle is a slate bed weighing-in at one ton which was built specifically for Queen Victoria.

15 Llangollen Railway

Locations: Llangollen and Carrog.
GPS: Llangollen: 52°58'13.39"N   3°10'13.14"W Carrog: 52°58'59.89"N 3°20'3.09"W.
OS map references: Llangollen: SJ215415. Carrog: SJ125425.
Operator: Llangollen Railway.
Contact details: Llangollen Railway, The Station, Abbey Road, Llangollen, Denbighshire, LL20 8SN. Telephone: 01978 860979. Fax: 01978 869247. E-mail: llangollen.railway@btinternet.com

Photographed from the A5 trunk road about two miles east of Glyndyfrdwy station on 25th April, 2009 is pannier tank No. 6430 'topped and tailed' by two autocoachs.   *Author*

Timetable: Consult the website or the talking timetable on 01978 860951

Route: Llangollen to Carrog, a distance of 7½ miles. There are plans to extend the line beyond Carrog almost to Corwen, albeit the old station there is no longer able to be used as it has been taken over by the local enterprise, Ifor Williams Trailers.

Journey time: Llangollen to Carrog takes 31 minutes and the return journey 33 minutes.

Traction: Steam locomotives which are operational include a Stanier 'Black Five' No. 44806, GWR pannier tank No. 6430, GWR 0-6-2T No. 5643, BR Standard class '4' 2-6-4T No. 80072, GWR 2-8-0 Heavy Freight No. 3802 and the saddle tank *Jesse*. Steam locomotives under refurbishment/reconstruction include GWR pannier tank No. 7754, GWR small prairie tanks Nos. 5532 and No. 5539, 0-4-0 tank No. 1498 *Desmond* (destined for the LMMR - *see entry 36)*, steam railmotor No. 93 (for the Great Western Society, Didcot), LMS 'Jinty' No. 7298 and No. 7822 *Foxcote Manor*. Diesel locomotives include Nos. 25313, 26010 (D5310), 37240, 47449 (D1566) and 46010. The Llangollen Railway is home to four sets of diesel-powered railcar classes '104', '108', '127', '105' and the unique Wickham pair - two-car dmu set. Of rolling stock interest is the Thompson buffet car originally built for the Kings Cross to Edinburgh 'Elizabethan' Express. This coach has been completed and is available for special events. A Thompson brake third is under reconstruction and will be rebuilt as a lounge vehicle to run in conjunction with the Thompson buffet. Autocoach No. 167 has been fully refurbished and is operational whilst autocoach No. 174, at the time of writing, is undergoing restoration at Pentrefelyn.

6880 - Betton Grange: A project is currently in hand to build new No. 6880 *Betton Grange*, there being no surviving member of this class of locomotive. In February 2010 the Board of 6880 Betton Grange (Society) Ltd announced that they had been successful in purchasing former GWR locomotive No. 5952 *Cogan Hall* together with a substantial amount of spares. *Cogan Hall* until recently was stored in the open at Llynclys on the Cambrian Heritage Railways. This acquisition will reduce the time and cost of constructing *Betton Grange*, although it may be 2015 before it is fully operational but follow the progress of this fascinating project on the website: www.6880.co.uk and contribute if one can. In the longer term it is intended to restore *Cogan Hall* to traffic as well.

Website: www.llangollen-railway.co.uk

Operating dates: Weekends throughout the year and on weekdays between June and October.

History of the original line: By the mid-19th century Llangollen had become a popular tourist attraction. A number of schemes were proposed to connect Llangollen to the railway network but the link was not made until the Vale of Llangollen Railway was opened to freight in 1861 and to passengers in 1862. This railway left the Shrewsbury to Chester line near Ruabon and travelled to Llangollen through Acrefair and Trevor, a distance of just over five miles. By the time this first section was being completed plans were already in hand to extend the line to Corwen. This connection was made by May 1865. Extension of the line further westwards was achieved to Llandrillo in 1866, Bala in 1868 and, later that same year, to Dolgellau. (NB: the former spelling until recently

On 27th February, 2005 a class '37' diesel leads a service back to Llangollen passing the locomotive works which can just be seen on the right. *Author*

GWR 2-8-0 Heavy Freight No. 3802 arriving at Carrog station in late winter snow on 4th March, 2006. *Author*

was Dolgelley or Dolgelly. Before the closure of the town's railway station all three versions could be found displayed there!) The final section to the coast at Barmouth was reached the following year. By 1896 all the founding railways had been absorbed into the Great Western Railway. By the end of the 1930s the route was already in decline. Along with many other railways in Britain the Beeching cuts in the 1960s took their toll with services on this overall route finally terminating in 1968. What a tragic end for what must have been a magnificent journey in its day, richly deserving the epithet 'God's Wonderful Railway'. To appreciate what it must have been like one can still follow the route (on the A494 for most of the way) where many of the structures still survive as if in some railway architectural graveyard, sad!

History of the restored railway: The revival of the railway line which serves the basis of this heritage railway began in 1972, four years after the final closure. A group of enthusiasts banded together to recreate a standard gauge railway in the region, their first choice being a site at Dyserth. Their subsequent experiences in developing what is now a very successful heritage railway are yet another object lesson in railway preservation. The story is well told on the railway's website at www.llangollen-railway.org.uk/page63.html

Railway constructions of interest: The Berwyn viaduct, the Berwyn tunnel, the Dee bridge and Llangollen, Glyndyfrdwy and Carrog stations.

What to see locally: Next to the railway station in Llangollen is the bridge over the River Dee built in 1347 and said to be one of the Seven Wonders of Wales. Llangollen is best known for its International Musical Eisteddfod which has taken place each July since 1948 although one was held as far as back as 1858. The modern event attracts as many as 120,000 visitors every year. The international event should not be confused with the National Eisteddfod which each year visits a different area of Wales. The Vale of Llangollen is perhaps one of the most scenic in Wales. The climb up to Crow Castle (w. *Castell Dinas Bran*) above Llangollen is a steep one but well worth the effort as the views are truly awesome.

Neighbouring railways: Bala Lake Railway.

Comments: Work has recently started to lay track for an extension from Carrog station towards Corwen Town, over a distance of 2½ miles further west.

16 Cambrian Heritage Railways

Locations: Llynclys and Oswestry in Shropshire on the Welsh border.

GPS: Oswestry: 52°51'35.70"N 3°3'13.24"W. Llynclys: 52°48'35.13"N 3°3'54.87"W. Pant: 52°47'33.09"N 3°4'36.34"W. Blodwel: 52°48'50.00"N 3°7'13.78"W.

OS map references: Llynclys: SJ281240. Oswestry: SJ289293.

Operators: Cambrian Railways Trust and Cambrian Railways Society in the process of combining to become Cambrian Heritage Railways Ltd.

Routes: At present there are two routes. The first, which is fully operational, is on a short stretch at Llynclys travelling south towards the village of Pant and terminating at Penygarreg Lane. The second, on which the work of recovery is well advanced, is off the main Shrewsbury to Chester line at Gobowen down to

Isabel heads back to Llynclys station on the last trip of the day on 2nd August, 2009.   *Author*

Oswestry station, a Grade II-listed building, is the former Cambrian Railways headquarters. It was opened in 1860 and finally closed in 1971.   *Author*

Blodwel Junction through Park Hall Halt, Oswestry station, Weston Wharf, Llynclys and Porthywaen Halt, a total distance of eight miles. After many years of complicated negotiations, this new route was confirmed in the spring of 2009, when lease agreements were concluded with Shropshire County Council.

Gauge: Standard.

Traction: A variety of interesting stock is held including the 1935-built GWR 'Hall' class No. 5952 *Cogan Hall* which very recently has been sold on to the 6880 - *Betton Grange* project at Llangollen (*see entry 15*). The mainstay of the steam services in 2009 was the 1919-built Hawthorn-Leslie 0-6-0 saddle tank No. 3437 *Isabel*. Latest information is that *Isabel* will not run in 2010 and may move to another railway. There are four Metro-Cammell dmus of late 1950s vintage and a collection of carriages.

Website: www.cambrianrailways.com

Operating dates: Diesel and steam services run at weekends between early April and late October. There are some specials at weekends on the run up to Christmas. Departures are at hourly intervals between 1100 and 1600 hours.

Tariff: A ticket is valid all day.

History of Cambrian Railways: The first railway to reach Oswestry was in 1848, with the arrival of a branch line off the Shrewsbury & Chester Railway from a junction created at Gobowen. The Shrewsbury & Chester Railway became part of the GWR in 1854. The Oswestry & Newtown Railway opened in 1860 operating from its own Oswestry station, a few yards from the GWR station. In the same year a branch line from Llynclys Junction to the quarry at Porthywaen was established. In 1863, the Oswestry, Ellesmere & Whitchurch Railway opened a line into Oswestry from the north. With the proliferation of individual railway companies it was not long before amalgamations took place. By 1865, the Oswestry & Newtown, the Oswestry, Ellesmere & Whitchurch Railway, the Newtown & Machynlleth Railway, the Llanidloes & Newtown Railway and the Aberystwyth & Welsh Coast Railway had combined to form the Cambrian Railways. Following the enactment of the Light Railways Act towards the end of the 19th century the Tanat Valley Light Railway was opened in 1904 as part of the Cambrian Railways network. In 1923, all the individual railway companies across the United Kingdom were grouped into one of the new 'Big Four' companies, Cambrian Railways being absorbed into an expanded Great Western Railway. In 1948, the railways were nationalized and the GWR became British Railways Western Region. A decline followed as the new British Railways sought the closure of uneconomic routes. During the 1950s the Tanat Valley line was progressively closed as was the main line from Whitchurch in the mid-1960s. The end finally came in November 1966 with the closure of passenger services on the Gobowen to Oswestry route. The line continued to move freight but even this came to an end in 1988. Fortunately, the line was officially 'mothballed' and the track not taken up which mercifully allows for today's intended revival. For more visit the Cambrian Heritage Railways website.

Railway constructions of interest: Oswestry station which is Grade II listed.

Whom to have known locally: Oswestry has its literary connections. World War I soldier and poet Lieutenant Wilfred Owen, MC (1893-1918) was born in Plas

Wilmot, a house near Oswestry. He was killed in action in the last week of the war at the Battle of Sambre, shot in the head as he crossed the Sambre-Oise Canal. He is probably best remembered for his war poems - *Dulce et Decorum Est, Insensibility, Anthem for Doomed Youth, Futility* and *Strange Meeting*. Educated at Oswestry School before going up to New College, Oxford and later ordained in the Church of England was William Archibald Spooner, the originator of 'spoonerisms'. These are plays on words in which corresponding consonants and vowels are switched. For example, attributed to him are 'Let us raise our glasses to the queer old Dean' (...dear old Queen), 'You have hissed all my mystery lectures, and were caught fighting a liar in the quad. Having tasted two worms, you will leave by the next town drain' (You have missed all my history lectures, and were caught lighting a fire in the quad. Having wasted two terms, you will leave by the next down train). He supposedly remarked to one lady, during a college reception, 'You'll soon be had as a matter of course' (You'll soon be mad as a Hatter of course); it is difficult to determine which was the most insulting!

What to see locally: Said to be one of the Seven Wonders of Wales is the 240 ft waterfall called *Pistyll Rhaeadr* (GPS: 52°52'23.76"N 3°23'5.49"W) near Llanrhaeadr-ym-Mochnant in Powys, 12 miles west of Oswestry.

Neighbouring railways: Llangollen Railway and, hopefully soon, the Glyn Valley Tramway.

The Future: Towards the end of 2009 the two separate organisations, given their close proximity with similar aims, met to explore the idea of working more closely together. After discussions a Joint Extraordinary General Meeting was held in November 2009 and the members agreed to bring the two organizations together under one body to be known as 'The Cambrian Heritage Railways Ltd'. At this stage this is not a merger as more needs to be done before assets can be transferred to the one company. It is thought that merger will help improve the new organization's standing in the local community and the railway preservation movement as well as help future applications for funding. It is believed that a final decision on a merger will be subject to a debate and vote at a future joint AGM/EGM. The overall aim continues to be 'Securing the restoration of the Cambrian Railways in order to preserve the unique railway heritage of Oswestry and to provide a visitor attraction of national significance'. The achievement of this aim has now taken a significant step forward with the leasing of the Gobowen (GPS: 52°53'47.74"N 3°2'12.11"W) to Blodwel route. Progress can now be made by the combined organizations to create a major heritage railway, which it is hoped will replicate the successful Llangollen Railway's experience by bringing significant numbers of new visitors to the Oswestry area every year. The Trust's short line at Llynclys saw steam trains working throughout the 2009 season and plans are already in hand to secure funding for extending these trains into Oswestry town, hopefully by 2012. With that in mind, Cambrian Heritage Railways have already requested Listed Buildings Consent for the re-building of a section of the platform at Oswestry station which will have the added benefit of significantly tidying this area of the town. Oswestry station is the former headquarters of Cambrian Railways; it is a listed building and has already seen significant investment for improvement.

The society's volunteers plan to run trains from Llynclys Junction towards Blodwel which will improve links to the historic Montgomery Canal, the Llanymynech Heritage Area, and other nearby attractions. The County Council are fully involved as exampled by their plans to construct a cycleway and footpath alongside parts of the restored railway track.

17 Bala Lake Railway

Location: Llanuwchllyn village off the A494, at the south-western end of Bala Lake (w. *Llyn Tegid)*.

GPS: Llanuwchllyn: 52°51′16.57″N   3°40′1.62″W.   Bala: 52°54′44.64″N 3°35′42.75″W.

OS map references: Llanuwchllyn: SH879305. Bala: SH923359.

Operator: Bala Lake Railway Ltd.

Contact details: The Station, Llanuwchllyn, Gwynedd, LL23 7DD. Telephone: 01678 540666. Fax: 01678 540535. E-mail: off the website or balalake@btconnect.com

Route: Llanuwchllyn to Bala (Pen-y-Bont Halt) via Pentrepiod, Llangower and Bryn Hynod, a distance of nine miles round trip.

Journey time: 25 minutes each way.

Gauge: Narrow (2 ft).

Website: www.bala-lake-railway.co.uk

Operating dates: On most days from April to the end of September but on Fridays and Mondays the railway is not normally operating except in July and August. There are Santa Specials in the first week in December. All trains start and finish their day at Llanuwchllyn with four return journeys per day. There are two services per day on mid-week days in April and October.

History: Bala Lake Railway occupies the trackbed of the former Great Western Railway route Ruabon to Barmouth line between the peaceful village of Llanuwchllyn and what was the Pen-y-Bont Halt on the southern side of Bala Lake (w. *Llyn Tegid)* and opposite to the market town of Bala.

Traction: There are five 0-4-0ST steam locomotives, four of which are ex-quarry engines from the Dinorwic slate quarry at Llanberis. The locomotives *Holy War, Maid Marian, Alice* and *George B* were built by the Hunslet Engine Company of Leeds at the beginning of the 20th century. The fifth, *Triassic,* is a Peckett & Sons locomotive built in Bristol in 1911 and was originally used by Rugby Portland Cement at Southam in Warwickshire.

Railway constructions of interest: Llanuwchllyn station.

What to see locally: Bala Lake is the largest natural body of water in Wales. It extends over 1,084 acres and is four miles long and one mile wide. It is subject to sudden and dangerous floods with heavy rain waters running off the mountains. It is of glacial origin and used to extend for some eight miles. It is crossed by the River Dee which on leaving the lake eventually drains into the Irish Sea beyond Chester. The lake now forms part of the River Dee regulation system to protect Chester and other locations downstream. The level of the outflow (w. *bala)* from the lake is automatically controlled causing water to flow either in to the lake or out depending on flow conditions.

Holy War, Hunslet Works No. 779, returns to Llanuwchllyn station on 22nd July, 2009. Built in 1902 it first went to the Dinorwic Slate Quarry. She was the last steam locomotive to work in a British slate quarry ending her duties at Dinorwic in November 1967. From there she went to Aylesbury for preservation and in 1975 she was purchased by a local Methodist Minister, the Revd Alan Cliff. Following an overhaul she entered passenger service on the Bala Lake Railway in 1979, and apart from a break for boiler repairs between 1985 and 1987 she has worked regularly ever since.   *Author*

The finely preserved and well-maintained Llanuwchllyn station as seen on 17th April, 2010. The original village here was swept away in a huge flood in 1781. It took three years to clear the debris from the lake.   *Author*

Neighbouring railways: Llangollen Railway.

Comments: Bala hosted the 2009 National Eisteddfod and was notable as the Bard's Chair unusually was not awarded to any of the entrants as the standard was deemed to be too low. The lake is popular for water sports. About 80 per cent of the population of Bala speak Welsh.

18 Ffestiniog Railway

Locations: Porthmadog and Blaenau Ffestiniog.

GPS: Porthmadog: 52°55'39.95"N 4°8'2.19"W. Blaenau Ffestiniog: 52°59'18.37"N 3°55'38.90"W.

OS map references: Porthmadog: SH565385. Blaenau Ffestiniog: SH695463.

Operator: Ffestiniog and Welsh Highland Railways.

Contact details: The Ffestiniog Railway, Harbour Station, Porthmadog, Gwynedd, LL49 9NF Telephone: 01766 516000 (General Enquiries), 01766 516024 (Booking Office). Fax: 01766 516005. E-mail: enquiries@festrail.co.uk

Route: Porthmadog to Blaenau Ffestiniog, Minffordd, Penrhyn (for Penrhyndeudraeth), Plas Halt. Tan-y-Bwlch through the Garnedd tunnel to Dduallt, the Moelwyn tunnel to Tanygrisiau to Blaenau Ffestiniog, total distance of 13½ miles. There are connections with main line rail services at Porthmadog, Minffordd and Blaenau Ffestiniog.

Journey time: About 1 hour 10 minutes each way.

Gauge: Narrow (2 ft).

Traction: Operational are an 1893-built Hunslet *Blanche*, 1992-built 'Double Fairlie' 0-4-4-0 *David Lloyd George*, 1979-built 'Double Fairlie' 0-4-4-0 *Earl of Merioneth*, 1879-built 'Double Fairlie' 0-4-4-0 *Merddin Emrys*, 1863/4-built by George England 0-4-0 *Palmerston*, 1863-built by George England *Prince*, and 1996/9 built 'Single Fairlie' 0-4-4 *Taliesin*. Out of traffic is *Linda* (but the good news is that she is expected to re-enter service in 2010-11) and *Mountaineer*. Extant are *Livingstone Thompson*, *Princess* and *Welsh Pony*. *Lilla* was non-operational but is now back in service. Finally there is a project ongoing to build a replica of one of the Manning, Wardle locomotives originally running on the Lynton & Barnstaple Railway in Devon. More on the project, which is about 80 per cent completed, is available on the website as is a gift aid form for those who wish to give financial support. The railway retains an interesting collection of carriages and other rolling stock dating from Victorian times to the modern day. See the 'carriages' section on the most informative website.

Website: www.festrail.co.uk

Operating dates: Services operate all the year round except in November. Trains operate a daily service between April and October and in December there are weekend operations with more on the run up to Christmas and New Year. In January and February trains run at weekends and also on some, but not all, Wednesdays and Thursdays. These involve 10-mile round trips to the viewing point at Trwyn-y-Garnedd from Porthmadog, leaving at 1315 hours. In February, the school half-term holidays are fully catered for. In March there are regular weekend services. Pre-booked coach parties are always possible. The limited winter service is dependent on necessary engineering possessions at the

Built by the Ffestiniog Railway at their Boston Lodge works is the 'Single Fairlie' 0-4-4 *Taliesin* here seen crossing the Cob on 25th January, 2009. *Author*

The 1992-built 'Double Fairlie' 0-4-4-0 *David Lloyd George* approaches Blaenau Ffestiniog on 24th July, 2009. *Author*

Ex-Penrhyn Quarry *Blanche* steams out on to the Cob on a winter Sunday service on 21st January, 2010.   *Author*

Boston Lodge Engineering Works (not open to the public) as photographed on 25th January, 2009.   *Author*

On 17th March, 2010 the 1992-built 'Double Fairlie' 0-4-4-0 *David Lloyd George* was caught here
near Tanygrisiau heading for Blaenau Ffestiniog.   *Author*

time. As with most heritage/tourist railways, the programme of events and timetables can change from year to year so it is wise to check the exact arrangements beforehand. Therefore, consult the comprehensive timetable/ tariff on the website for more information and/or telephone the booking office on 01766 516024.

Tariff: All-day rovers are available. Dogs and bicycles may be carried for a flat fee of £2.50.

History of the route: The Ffestiniog Railway, founded by an Act of Parliament in 1832, is the oldest independent railway company in the world. The railway was originally built to transport slate from the quarries around Blaenau Ffestiniog where there is still considerable amount of evidence of the mine workings. As the demand for slate increased so the railway grew as did the town of Porthmadog. Slates from Blaenau Ffestiniog were sent to all over the world on ships, some of which were built in Porthmadog. Not only did Welsh slate make an impact throughout the world, the railway did as well for many engineers came from afar to study what had been achieved. As a consequence, the Ffestiniog Railway has influenced the design and construction of railways in many locations throughout the world. As elsewhere, the demand for real slate diminished and so the industry slowly declined. Eventually, in 1946, the railway was closed to freight and with it went passenger traffic.

History of today's Ffestiniog Railway: It was six years after the end of World War II that a small group met in Bristol to discuss the feasibility of resurrecting the railway. In 1954, Alan Pegler (of *Flying Scotsman* fame) donated his controlling interest in the business to the Ffestiniog Railway Trust and so began the long journey to recovery. In 1955, a passenger service crossed 'the Cob' (explained later) to Boston Lodge (not accessible to visitors). Easter 1957 saw trains run to Penrhyn (for Penrhyndeudraeth) and the following Easter to Tan-y-Bwlch. However a major obstruction was encountered when the then British Electricity Authority (BEA) acquired a compulsory purchase order to buy land on part of the route to Blaenau Ffestiniog. The BEA plan was to develop a hydro-electric scheme near Tanygrisiau and despite objections the construction went ahead. The consequence was that there was no future for a route beyond this point. Not to be thwarted the railway decided, with some monies gained in compensation, to introduce a large loop to run round the man-made lake on land donated by the Economic Forestry Group. This became known as 'The Great Deviation'. By 1970, a new route had been agreed and the next year the Dduallt spiral was completed. There followed the Moelwyn tunnel in 1977 and the following year the connection to the original route path was achieved. There followed what the enthusiasts will remember as the 'slog' to Blaenau Ffestiniog with that goal achieved by May 1982. The completed line was officially opened in the May of the following year by the then Speaker of the House of Commons, The Rt Hon. George Thomas, MP for Cardiff West and later 1st Viscount Tonypandy. The Ffestiniog Railway has flourished ever since and is soon to achieve an exciting development when the railway meets the sister Welsh Highland Railway at Porthmadog.

What to see locally: Porthmadog is a gateway to Snowdonia. Arriving from the south one enters the town along the famous 'Cob' which was built to form the deep harbour from where great sailing ships carried the slate mined in Blaenau Ffestiniog to all over the world. The Cob carries the road and the railway with a footpath running alongside from which, to the north and to the east is the wide expanse of the Glaslyn estuary. This is well known to ornithologists as an important location for migrating birds and wildlife generally.

Neighbouring railways: Welsh Highland Heritage Railway (closer to the main line station in Porthmadog), the Welsh Highland Railway (at present reaching Hafod y Llyn near Beddgelert but progressing towards Porthmadog), Llanberis Lake Railway and the Snowdon Mountain Railway. The railway connects at Blaenau Ffestiniog station with the Arriva train services from Llandudno Junction on the Conwy Valley Railway and at Minffordd on the Porthmadog to Machynlleth route.

Comments: Over the past 50 years, the Ffestiniog Railway has become a renowned world leader in railway preservation and is now one of the top tourist attractions in the whole of Wales. NB: The engineering works for the railway are at Boston Lodge but public visits are definitely not possible, not least for health and safety reasons.

Blanche leaves Porthmadog station on 21st January, 2010.   *Author*

19 Welsh Highland Railway (WHR)

Locations: Caernarfon and Hafod y Llyn.
GPS: Caernarfon: 53°8'42.40"N 4°16'7.45"W. (Hafod y Llyn) near Beddgelert: 53°0'42.26"N 4°5'56.61"W.
OS map references: Caernarfon: SH485625. Hafod y Llyn: SH599457.
Operator: Ffestiniog & Welsh Highland Railways.
Contact details: Welsh Highland Railway, Harbour Station, Porthmadog, Gwynedd, LL49 9NF. Telephones: 01766 516000 for general enquiries and 01766 516024 for the Porthmadog booking office (open all year); 01286 677018 for the Caernarfon booking office (limited winter opening). Fax: 01766 516005. E-mail: enquiries@festrail.co.uk
Route: Caernarfon to Hafod y Llyn (reached by 2009) via Bontnewydd, Dinas (opened 1997), Waunfawr (2000), Plas y Nant, Snowdon Ranger, Rhyd Ddu (2003), Meillionen (Forest Campsite), Beddgelert (2009) and Aberglaslyn Pass (2009). By 2011 it is hoped to reach Porthmadog with proposed future halts at Nantmor before Hafod y Llyn and beyond at Pont Croesor and Pen-y-Mount. The total distance from Caernarfon to Porthmadog will be just short of 25 miles.
Journey time: Caernarfon to Hafod y Llyn currently takes 1 hr 50 min.
Gauge: Narrow (2 ft).
Traction: Services on this line in the main are operated by a set of four Beyer-Garratt NGG16 (2-6-2 + 2-6-2) locomotives formerly deployed in South Africa. They are considered to be the most powerful engines operating on this gauge in the world. Such power is not misplaced as the trains with up to 10 coaches (the maximum number that can be accommodated on Caernarfon platform) have to negotiate challenging gradients of up to 1 in 40 on this route. The locomotives can travel up to 25 mph thus permitting practical journey times. The locomotives are heavy, weighing-in at 62 tons; they are big, each being 48 ft in length; they have huge carrying capacities, i.e. 1,500 gallons of water and in excess of four tons of coal, if that were to be the fuel carried. They are ideal for the mountainous terrain for their two powered bogies help provide adhesion in the most slippery of conditions. The main benefit of these locomotives designed by Herbert William Garratt was that the boiler and firebox were freed from size constraints by being between the two engine units rather than over the frames and running gear. This allowed for boilers to be of greater diameter thus increasing the heated area and the more fuel-efficient production of steam. The main disadvantage of the Garratt design is one shared with tank engines in that adhesion aided by weight is reduced as the water and fuel are consumed. However, to overcome this, a wagon containing water was attached to the locomotive which also had the added benefit of allowing longer operating distances. Of WHR's Garratts, No. 138 arrived in 1997 and at first operated in dark green livery but was repainted to a lighter green in 2001 and named *Mileniwm/Millennium* the following year. No. 143, sporting black livery, also arrived on the line in 1997 and went into service towards the end of the 1998 season after significant boiler repairs had been completed in Lancashire. The third, NGC16 is No. 140, nicknamed the 'Red Devil' because of her bright red livery, was donated to the railway by a group of German and Swiss enthusiasts.

Beyer-Garrett NGG16 No. 87, built by Cockerill of Belgium (in a temporary photographic grey livery) descends from Rhyd Ddu heading for Snowdon Ranger on 24th July, 2009. Snowdon in cloud offers the backdrop. *Author*

Diesel locomotive *Vale of Ffestiniog* runs alongside the river as it approaches the Aberglaslyn valley on 24th July, 2009. The valley (OS ref: SH595455) is said to be the most photographed in the whole of Wales for its outstanding beauty. *Author*

Nos. 138, 140 and 143 were all built by Beyer, Peacock of Manchester in 1958 and all are fuelled by oil. Given they are all similar these locomotives allow WHR operations to continue uninterrupted by a planned programme of 'boiler-swapping'. No. 87, fuelled by oil, was built by John Cockerill in Belgium in 1935 and was acquired by the WHR in 2006. When last seen by the author it was finished in 'photographic grey' but it is believed that it will eventually carry South African Railways black livery. In addition to the four Garratts just described, there is also No. K1, which was also built by Beyer, Peacock of Manchester over a hundred years ago. K1, constructed to the Garratt patent, also saw service south of the equator in Tasmania on the North East Dundas Tramway, a branch line between Zeehan and Williamsford. Eventually K1 made her way back to Manchester and was subsequently purchased by the Ffestiniog Railway in 1966. Much work has been undertaken to return K1 to operations which was successfully achieved in 2007. Incidentally, Pete Waterman has purchased an NGG16 - No. 109 - which will be restored at the London & North Western Railway workshops in Crewe with a view to it eventually entering service on the WHR. Finally there are two 'Funkey' diesels which were purchased from South Africa in 1993, one for the WHR, named *Castell Caernarfon* and the other, which has been significantly rebuilt, was named *Vale of Ffestiniog* for the Ffestiniog Railway although it was last seen by the author working on the WHR as illustrated here.

Rolling stock: There are a number and variety of coaches including heritage coach No. 23 (in green 1920s WHR livery) heritage coach No. 24 (in red NWNGR livery) seven third class saloons and one brake saloon, three third class semi-open coaches, two bike carrying wagons and two brake vans. There is also a magnificent 20-seat first class 'Pullman' coach, No. 2115, completed in 1998 by Winson Engineering. Generous sponsorship from Historic Houses Hotels Ltd (HHH) has allowed for the provision of a luxury interior. In recognition of that donation the coach carries the name *Bodysgallen* which is the name of one of the HHH hotels in Llandudno. More recently a new observation Pullman coach, No. 2100, entered service in 2009 and a service car, No. 2010, which had become operational the year before.

Website: www.festrail.co.uk

Operating dates: Services operate from April to October each year and also Christmas/New Year specials are offered. Up to five services operate each way on the busiest days of the season and one each way on the quietest. The timetable is published on the excellent website along with the helpful 'Loco Roster' indicating a few days in advance the specific locomotives intended (but not guaranteed) to be in service.

History of the route: The origins of what eventually has become the Welsh Highland Railway can be traced back to a number of narrow gauge railway developments including the Nantlle Tramway (1828), the Croesor Tramway (1864) which later, in 1901, became the Porthmadog, Beddgelert & South Snowdon Railway (PBSSR) and, finally, perhaps the best known to railway historians, the NWNGR - North Wales Narrow Gauge Railways (1877-1881). In 1914, the local authorities proposed a Light Railway Order with the intention of taking over the PBSSR and NWNGR and completing the railway. In 1922 an

Beyer-Garrett NGG16 No. 87 continues is descent through staggeringly beautiful countryside from Rhyd Ddu and about to pass the waters of Llwn Cwellyn on 24th July, 2009.   *Author*

'Funkey' diesel *Vale of Ffestiniog* emerges from the Aberglaslyn valley on 24th July, 2009.

Author

Order was made to create the Welsh Highland Railway, construction began and the following year the entire route was opened. Unfortunately the WHR struggled from the outset and went into receivership in 1927. Thereafter attempts were made to keep the line operating but these came to an end after the conclusion of World War II. For an interesting and comprehensive account of the history of this railway (from which this brief description was sourced) visit the history pages on the railway's website.

History of today's WHR: As with the Ffestiniog Railway this is a tale of perseverance. The early 1960s saw the first serious efforts to revive the WHR. In 1961, a society of enthusiasts became the Welsh Highland Light Railway (1964) Co. Ltd. Negotiations followed over the years which were both long-running and complex not least with the Official Receiver in London and others including the neighbouring Ffestiniog Railway. In 1993, the Ffestiniog Railway formed a Welsh Highland Railway Society focusing efforts on the reconstruction of the line. Several years of legal arguments followed including three public inquiries. Success, however, followed and by 1997 work began on the trackbed between Dinas and Caernarfon and by the October of that year the first trains travelled this section of the route. An extension of the track to Waunfawr and Rhyd Ddu followed. Meanwhile the Welsh Highland Light Railway (1964) Co. Ltd, now the Welsh Highland Railway Ltd and operating as the Welsh Highland Heritage Railway (*see next entry*) came to an agreement with Ffestiniog Railway to rebuild the railway to Pont Croesor and operate trains until this section was required for the completion of the overall route to Porthmadog's harbour station. In September 2004, funding was forthcoming from the Welsh Assembly and the European Union to allow for the extension of the railway from Rhyd Ddu through Beddgelert and Aberglaslyn to Porthmadog. Work began in 2005 and by the beginning of the 2009 season, Beddgelert (originally opened in 1905) and the route through the Aberglaslyn Pass (GPS: 52°59'51.01"N 4°5'40.26"W. OS: Aberglaslyn SH595455) to Hafod y Llyn had become operational for public services (albeit passengers could not alight at Hafod y Llyn). Work continues with the intention that the line will be fully completed in 2011 a tribute to the hard work and determination of all those involved over the many years. To fully appreciate the trials and tribulations read the parts 4 and 5 of the fascinating history on the website pages.

Railway constructions of interest: The magnificent mountain route itself, a credit to the enthusiasts over the years. Incidentally, the Aberglaslyn Pass is said to be the most photographed location in the whole of Wales; in the opinion of the author, it is now much improved by the addition of the railway.

What to see locally: The imposing Caernarfon Castle is arguably the most famous of Wales's fortresses. Its construction as a military stronghold, seat of government and royal palace was begun in 1283 as part of Edward I's conquest of Wales. Caernarfon's royal status was established when Edward ensured that his son, the first English Prince of Wales, was born there in 1284. The castle was the setting for the Investiture of Prince Charles as the current Prince of Wales in 1969. Standing at the mouth of the River Seiont, the castle dominates the walled town. The castle houses the Regimental Museum of Wales's oldest regiment the Royal Welch Fusiliers.

What to know locally: The village of Beddgelert (GPS: 53°0'42.63"N 4°5'57.84"W. OS: SH595485) is famed for the tragic story of Prince Llywelyn ab Iorwerth and his dog. The Prince went hunting and left his infant son in the protective charge of his faithful dog Gelert. On his return, Llywelyn on being greeted by Gelert noticed the dog's muzzle was red with blood; his son was nowhere to be seen. Llywelyn, thinking the worst, attacked the dog, and it fell to the ground gravely injured. Within minutes he heard a child's cry and stumbled through nearby undergrowth to find his son, unharmed in his cradle. Beside the cradle lay the body of a giant wolf covered in wounds, obviously the result of a fight to the death with Gelert. Llywelyn returned to his faithful dog to see it die from the wounds he had inflicted. It is said that Llywelyn never smiled again. If this story brings a tear to one's eye, fret not, as the story, as it turns out, is pure fiction concocted by local traders, probably in the 19th century, keen to entice visitors to the village! The truth of the matter is that Gelert was a local sixth century saint whose grave (w. *bedd*) supposedly made up of a slab lying on its side with two upright stones standing in a beautiful meadow below Cerrig Llan.

What to find locally: Gold! At the Sygun Copper mine, abandoned in 1903, audiovisual tours allow visitors safely to explore the old mine workings on foot. The winding tunnels take the visitor to large, colourful chambers with imposing stalactite and stalagmite formations and veins of copper ore which contain traces of gold, silver and other precious metals.

Neighbouring railways: The Ffestiniog Railway, Llanberis Lake Railway, the Welsh Highland Heritage Railway and the Snowdon Mountain Railway.

Comments: When Porthmadog is eventually reached in 2011, this railway will connect with the Ffestiniog Railway and then be offering a superb route of over 38 miles of 'Great Railway Journey' making it, in the author's opinion, one of the best in Europe. This is already a 'must-do' railway and will be even more so soon. Follow the progress on the website.

The *Vale of Ffestiniog* diesel heads its train back from Hafod y Llyn towards the Aberglaslyn valley on 24th July, 2009.   *Author*

20 Welsh Highland Heritage Railway

Location: Porthmadog.
GPS: 52°55′39.95″N 4°8′2.19″W.
OS map reference: Porthmadog station: SH565391.
Operator: Welsh Highland Heritage Railway (WHHR), known until February 2009 as the Welsh Highland Railway (Porthmadog). The parent name is the Welsh Highland Railway Ltd.
Contact details: Welsh Highland Heritage Railway, Tremadog Road, Porthmadog LL49 9DY. Telephone: 01766 513402. E-mail: info@whr.co.uk
Route: Porthmadog (WHHR station at the top of the High Street near to the main line station) to Pen-y-Mount and Traeth Mawr loop, a distance of about one mile.
Gauge: Narrow (2 ft).
Steam Traction: A Peckett 0-4-2T *Karen*, a Quarry Hunslet 0-4-2T *Lady Madcap* being restored from the frames up, a 1906-built Hunslet 2-6-2T *Russell* restored in 1987 but now in need of boiler work and other maintenance. A Baldwin, No. 794, is on long-term loan from the Imperial War Museum at Duxford. When funds permit, it will be reconstructed as No. 590. There is also a selection of diesel-powered traction including in service *Glaslyn* and *Kinnerley* both built by Ruston & Hornsby in the early 1950s and *Eryri* built in Romania in 1977.
Website: www.whr.co.uk
Operating dates: Late March to the end of October with departures at 1030, 1130, 1300, 1400, 1500 and, except in October, 1600 hours
Tariff: A ticket is valid all day.

The Bagnall 0-4-2T *Gelert* approaches the WHHR station on 30th October, 2005.

Author

Passenger launch *Snowdon Star*, of 1947 vintage, provides a ferry service between Llanberis and the Padarn Country Park. Just visible in the distance is Hunslet-built (ex-Dinorwic Quarries) *Elidir* running along the north-eastern side of Llyn Padarn on 29th March, 2009.   *Author*

Elidir heads a service out from Llanberis station towards Gilfach Ddu on 29th March, 2009.
     Author

Neighbouring railways: The Ffestiniog Railway, the North Wales Coast route to Holyhead and the Cambrian lines from Porthmadog and soon to arrive in Porthmadog the Welsh Highland Railway.

Comments: Trains leave the WHHR station and travel out to Pen-y-Mount where the train turns round and returns to the station stopping off at the engine sheds on the way. These sheds were doubled in size in 2009 to provide an interesting interactive museum about the small railways of the area. It is understood that by a 1998 agreement the Ffestiniog Railway Company and the Welsh Highland Railway will have running rights over the completed WHR line perhaps from Caernarfon to Porthmadog but exactly what this means for the WHHR is at the time of writing unclear.

21 Llanberis Lake Railway

Location: Llanberis.

GPS: Llanberis: 53°7′8.72″N 4°7′49.11″W.

OS map reference: Llanberis: SH575605.

Operator: Llanberis Lake Railway (*w. Rheilffordd Llyn Padarn*) Ltd.

Contact details: Llanberis Lake Railway (Rheilffordd Llyn Padarn), Gilfach Ddu, Llanberis, Caernarfon, Gwynedd, LL55 4TY. Telephone: 01286 870549. Email: info@lake-railway.co.uk

Route: Llanberis via Gilfach Ddu to Penllyn via Cei Llydan, a distance of five miles round trip.

Journey time: About 60 minutes round trip.

Gauge: Narrow (1 ft 11½ in).

Traction: Three Hunslet 0-4-0ST locomotives are maintained. The first is *Wild Aster* of 1904 - which has operated as *Thomas Bach* (meaning 'Little Thomas' - nickname for one of the regular quarry drivers) for most of its service with the railway. *Wild Aster* plates were restored in summer 2009 to mark 40 years since the Dinorwic quarry closed. At present the locomotive carries one *Wild Aster* and one *Thomas Bach* nameplate. The other two Hunslets are *Elidir* of 1889 vintage - originally named *Enid*, but for most of its quarry life was known as *Red Damsel*; and finally *Dolbadarn* built in 1922. There are also four diesel locomotives, all Rustons, three of which are in service). Occasionally the railway permits *Una* (also a Hunslet 0-4-0ST) from the Welsh Slate Museum onto the line via the connecting siding between the museum and the railway.

Website: www.lake-railway.co.uk

Operating dates: The operating season now runs from mid-February (half-term) until early December plus Santa Trains in the run-up to Christmas. Services are operated daily (or virtually daily - check first) from March to October.

History: The Llanberis Lake Railway is built on part of the trackbed of the 4 ft gauge Padarn Railway, which from 1843 carried slate from the Dinorwic Quarry down to Port Dinorwic situated on the Menai Strait. The quarry was closed in 1961 and the rolling stock and track were sold for scrap. The first two miles lay alongside the attractive lake, Llyn Padarn, which gave rise to thoughts at the time of developing the route as a tourist railway. Initially a mile of narrow gauge track

That Jack Russell terrier again, this time watching Llanberis Railway's *Elidir* crossing the road near Gilfach Ddu visitor centre on 29th March, 2009.   *Author*

was laid. Three steam engines and one diesel locomotive were purchased from the Dinorwic Quarry and the gauge modified to 1 ft 11½ in. The railway first opened in 1971 and the following year the line was extended along the two mile length of the lake. In June 2003 a useful extension of the line was made to the village of Llanberis opposite the terminus of the Snowdon Mountain Railway.

What to see locally: The 13th century Dolbadarn Castle, half a mile south of Llanberis, is an ideal vantage point to observe the railway and lake. From here there are stunning views of the 3,560 ft (1,085 m.) high Snowdon mountain, the highest peak in Wales. Set in the magnificent scenery of Snowdonia is 'Electric Mountain' which is the company First Hydro's visitor centre in Llanberis. In a split level building there is a gift shop and café and also the starting point for the tour of Dinorwig power station. Admission to the visitor centre is free but there is a charge for the hour-long tour of the power station. From the visitor centre, a First Hydro bus (which gives one some indication of the scale of the power station operation) transports visitors on the site. As First Hydro publicity says 'Descending deep inside ancient Elidir mountain's labyrinth of dark and imposing tunnels, visitors will experience one of man's greatest engineering achievements … It's electrifying!' (NB: Cameras, mobile phones, handbags, rucksacks and so on are not allowed on the tour but lockers are provided for their safe-keeping.)

Neighbouring railways: Welsh Highland Railway, Welsh Highland Heritage Railway and the Ffestiniog Railway. The Snowdon Mountain railway terminus is across the road from this railway in the village of Llanberis.

Comments: All trains offer wheelchair accommodation, but spaces are limited, so it is advisable to pre-book. Toilets, which include disabled access, are situated nearby in the Padarn Country Park.

22 Snowdon Mountain Railway

Location: Llanberis.
GPS: Llanberis: 53°7'8.72"N 4°7'49.11"W.
OS map reference: Llanberis: SH575605.
Operator: Heritage Attractions Limited, Suite 37, The Colonnades, Albert Dock, Liverpool, L3 4AA.
Contact details: Snowdon Mountain Railway *(w. Rheilffordd yr Wyddfa)* Llanberis, Gwynedd LL55 4TY. Fax: 01286 872518. Booking telephone hotline: 0844 493 8120. E-mail: info@snowdonrailway.co.uk
Route: Llanberis to Snowdon Summit (GPS: 53°5'15.64"N 4°5'4.11"W) via Hebron, Halfway, Rocky Valley and Clogwyn station, a total length of 4 miles and 1,188 yards.
Journey time: The return journey to the summit station (the highest in Great Britain) takes 2½ hours which includes a 30 minute stop at the top. If the train terminates at Clogwyn station, which sometimes is necessary because of adverse weather conditions, then the return journey takes two hours.
Gradient: The average gradient on the route is 1 in 7.86 with the steepest section being 1 in 5.5. These gradients demand a rack and pinion system to provide traction as normal adhesion will not suffice. Incidentally, the Snowdon Mountain Railway is the only publicly-operated rack and pinion railway in the British Isles.
Gauge: The rack and pinion system used on the railway is that designed by the Swiss mechanical engineer Carl Roman Abt (1850-1933). Abt at the time was working on a rack/cogwheel railway utilizing the system designed by Carl Riggenbach; he thought that Riggenbach's system could be much improved. The Abt rack features steel plates mounted vertically and in parallel to the rails, with rack teeth machined to a precise profile within them. These engage with the locomotive's pinion teeth much more smoothly than the Riggenbach system. Two or three parallel sets of Abt rack plates are used, with a corresponding number of driving pinions on the locomotive which ensures that at least one pinion tooth is always securely engaged. Incidentally, the first use of the Abt system was on the Harzbahn in Germany which opened in 1885. The Abt system is now the most popular in use in the world. For more on rack railways read the author's *Essential Guides* on Switzerland and on Austria (*see Bibliography*). The railway with a gauge of 2 ft 7½ in. which is the one found on most mountain railways, is single track with three passing points, i.e. at Hebron (alt. 1,069 ft - 326 m.), Halfway (alt. 1,641 ft - 500 m.) and Clogwyn (alt. 2,556 ft - 779 m.). The average speed of the trains is 5 mph.
Traction and rolling stock: Four coal-fired locomotives, named *Enid, Wyddfa, Snowdon* and *Padarn*, were built by SLM of Winterthur in Switzerland. Three of these were built between 1895 and 1896 with the fourth constructed in 1922. Three other steam locomotives, named *Moel Siabod, Ralph* and *Eryri*, are out of service. There are four British-built (Hunslet of Leeds) diesel locomotives to support the steam locomotives; named *Ninian, Yeti, Peris* and *George*, they were constructed between 1986 and 1992. The boilers on the steam locomotives are unlike those of a traditional steam locomotive in that they are

Rack steam locomotive No. 4 *Snowdon* on 29th March, 2009 pushes its passenger carriage across the viaduct over the Afon Hwch before reaching the waterfall. *Author*

Diesel-powered rack locomotive No. 11 *Peris* pushes its carriage with a full complement of passengers towards Hebron on 29th March, 2009. *Author*

inclined to allow the boiler tubes and the firebox to remain lower when on a gradient, a standard practice on all mountain railways. For safety reasons, the locomotive always pushes the train up the mountain and leads it down with a single carriage in front which is not coupled to the locomotive. Additional to the fleet are three diesel-electric railcars built in the mid-1990s by HPE Tredegar Ltd of South Wales. There are six carriages built by the Lancaster Carriage & Wagon Co. Ltd in 1895, two by Schweizerische Industrie-Gesellschaft of Neuhausen in Switzerland in 1923 and one by East Lancashire Coach Builders Ltd of Blackburn in 1987. The original carriages were open above the waist but did have canvas curtains. Between 1951 and 1957 these carriages were modified by Hunslet of Leeds to provide enclosed bodies to afford better protection to the passengers from the elements which can be difficult at any time of the year.

Website: www.snowdonrailway.co.uk

Operating dates: Services operate for eight months of the year but not from the beginning of November to mid-March when maintenance programmes are undertaken during a period when weather conditions deny operations. The first train of the day is normally 0900 hours with frequent services thereafter.

Tariff: Those who book at least one day in advance for the 0900 hours departure, travel at half price.

History: In 1869, a branch line of the London & North Western Railway opened from Caernarfon to Llanberis to transport visitors to the foot of Snowdon. Thereafter, the only way to reach the summit was on foot or by donkey! Thoughts soon turned towards the building of a railway to the top. A local landowner, George William Duff Assherton-Smith, believed that such a railway would desecrate the scenery so he rejected every proposal submitted for the following 20 years! However, the spirit of competition came to the rescue when a rival plan was mooted to build a railway to the summit from the southern side of the mountain at Rhyd Ddu. This ignited fears that Llanberis would lose its tourist trade which prompted Assherton-Smith to have a major rethink. Subsequently he agreed to allow his land to be used and on 16th November, 1894 the Snowdon Mountain Tramroad & Hotels Co. Ltd was established to construct the railway. Ground-breaking took place at Llanberis station in December 1894. It had been intended that the railway would be ready for summer of 1895. However, the preceding especially harsh winter delayed the building, particularly of the two large viaducts between Llanberis and the waterfall. As a consequence these structures took much longer than expected and were not completed until August 1895. Once the viaducts were in place the laying of the remaining track to the summit took place remarkably quickly, in fact in just 72 days. The first train reached the summit in January 1896. With the finalisation of work on fencing and signals the railway formally opened to the public at Easter 1896.

What to remember: Sadly, the opening was marred by a tragic accident. On Monday 6th April, 1896, locomotive No. 2 *Enid* had travelled to the summit to check for boulders on the line. On its return No. 1 *Ladas* departed with two carriages on the first official train. *Enid* followed with a second train. On its return down the mountain the driver had difficulty in controlling the speed of

Steam-powered rack locomotive No. 3 *Wyddfa* on the way up the lower slopes of Snowdon on 29th March, 2009. The lake, Llyn Padarn, and the village of Llanberis are in the background. *Author*

No. 2, the steam-powered rack locomotive *Enid*, being prepared for the day's work on 29th March, 2009. *Author*

the descent. About half a mile above Clogwyn, *Ladas* jumped off the rack rail. It continued running on and down the track, but now the driver had no ability to stop the speeding train. The driver and the fireman jumped from the footplate. As luck would have it the automatic brakes were applied on the carriages (triggered at 7-10 mph) and brought the carriages safely to a halt. Unfortunately, before the carriages had stopped, a passenger, Ellis Griffith Roberts of Llanberis, having seen the driver and fireman jump, did the same and suffered a serious cut to his head later dying from loss of blood. To compound matters, *Ladas* had severed the telegraph lines denying communication with the summit station to stop *Enid* making her descent. As a consequence *Enid* did exactly the same thing, losing the rack rail and eventually ploughing into *Ladas'* carriages. These carriages ran on down the gradient and came to halt when they derailed. The impact with the carriages however caused *Enid* to drop back on to the rack rail and stop safely.

What to know and see locally: Snowdon in Welsh is *Yr Wyddfa*, which means 'great tomb' allegedly derived from a legend which says that a great giant was slain by King Arthur and was buried on the summit. The rugged natural beauty of Llanberis Pass is a most popular resort for serious walkers and is equally enjoyable for those travelling by cycle or by car.

Neighbouring railways: Welsh Highland Heritage Railway, Welsh Highland Railway and the Llanberis Lake Railway.

Comments: At the summit of Snowdon is *Hafod Eryri*, the fairly recent Visitor Centre, controversial to some. *Eryri* is the Welsh name for Snowdonia and literally means 'Land of Eagles'. (NB: Only officially registered dogs for the disabled are allowed on the trains. Disabled passengers may be carried subject to discussions before travelling preferably well in advance if not to be disappointed.)

23 Cambrian Lines - Pwllheli to Porthmadog

Locations: Pwllheli and Porthmadog
GPS: Pwllheli: 52°53'14.54"N 4°25'32.11"W. Porthmadog: 52°55'39.95"N 4°8'2.19"W.
OS map references: Pwllheli: SH378347. Porthmadog station: SH565391.
Operator: Arriva Trains Wales.
Timetable: Arriva No. 1.
Route: Pwllheli to Porthmadog via Aberach, Penychain, and Criccieth.
Journey time: 33 minutes.
Website: www.arrivatrainswales.co.uk
Operating dates: Daily with eight services each way.
What to know locally: The British Prime Minister, David Lloyd George grew up in the village of Llanystumdwy, near Criccieth. He is buried in the church's graveyard. Tremadog, north-west of Porthmadog, was the birthplace of T.E. Lawrence (of Arabia fame) in 1888. The house where he was born was originally called 'Gorphwysfa' before being given the English name of 'Woodlands'. Later it reverted to the original name but more recently has been changed to 'Lawrence House'.

An Arriva train passes Criccieth beach. The photograph is taken from below Criccieth's 13th century castle on 17th January, 2010. *Author*

On 6th August, 2009 two Arriva class '158' dmus pass at Harlech station. *Author*

What to see locally: Pwllheli is said to be the unofficial capital of the beautiful Lleyn Peninsula. Criccieth, which styles itself as 'The Pearl of Wales on the Shores of Snowdonia', has an early 13th castle which featured significantly in the wars between the Welsh and the English. The imposing twin-towered gatehouse is believed to have been the original stronghold of Llywelyn ab Iorwerth, although some historians claim it for Edward I. Criccieth bay was one of the locations used by J.M.W. Turner (painter of *Rain, Steam and Speed - The Great Western Railway*) for his famous series on shipwrecked mariners.

Neighbouring railways: Ffestiniog Railway, Welsh Highland Heritage Railway, Welsh Highland Railway and the Llanberis Lake Railway.

24 Cambrian Lines - Porthmadog to Machynlleth

Locations: Porthmadog and Machynlleth.
GPS: Porthmadog: 52°55'39.95"N 4°8'2.19"W. Machynlleth: Machynlleth: 52°35'30.97"N 3°51'9.89"W.
OS map reference: Porthmadog station: SH565391. Machynlleth: SH748012.
Operator: Arriva Trains Wales.
Timetable: Arriva No. 1.
Route: Porthmadog to Machynlleth via Minffordd (for Portmeiron) Penrhyndeudraeth, Llandecwyn, Talsarnau, Tygwyn, Harlech, Llandanwg, Pensarn, Llanbedr, Dyffryn Ardudwy, Talybont, Llanaber, Barmouth, Morfa Mawddach, Fairbourne, Llwyngwril, Tonfanau, Tywyn, Aberdovey and Penhelg, a distance of about 61 miles.
Journey time: 1 hour 46 minutes.
Website: www.arrivatrainswales.co.uk
Operating dates: Daily with services every two hours.
Railway constructions of interest: Without doubt the Barmouth bridge (GPS: 52°43'13.15"N 4°2'51.33"W) is one to see. The bridge (w. *Pont Abermaw*) is a single-track largely wooden-constructed railway viaduct which was built by the Aberystwyth and Welsh Coast Railway and opened in 1867. It crosses the estuary of the Afon Mawddach between the hamlet of Morfa Mawddach near Fairbourne and the town of Barmouth. A footpath runs alongside the railway and pedestrians can cross the river on payment of a toll, the ticket given being valid all day. The distance is about 900 yards. Originally the bridge included a lifting drawbridge made of wood to allow the passage of tall ships but this was replaced in 1901 as a swing bridge with two steel spans. Passenger train services over the bridge reduced significantly in the 1960s, when the Ruabon to Barmouth line via Llangollen (*see entry 15*) and Dolgellau was closed causing all traffic to take the longer and slower route from Shrewsbury via Machynlleth and Dovey Junction. Concerns were raised in 1980 about the safety of the ageing wooden structure caused by marine worm damage. The weight of modern traction led to an immediate ban on locomotive-hauled trains which effectively saw the end of the local freight traffic. Repairs were undertaken five years later and the weight restriction was relaxed in 2005. Since then locomotive-hauled trains have been allowed to cross, including steam-hauled specials as is depicted in the photographs (*see page 90*).

BR Standard class '4MT' No. 76079 crosses Barmouth bridge on 7th August, 2009 hauling 'The Cambrian' service for the West Coast Railway Company. In July 1974 this locomotive was the fifty-ninth to be rescued from the Barry scrapyard.   *Author*

'The Cambrian' steam special in 2009 deploying BR Standard class '4MT' No. 76079. The train is seen entering Barmouth on 7th August, 2009.   *Caroline Jones*

What to do locally: Walk or cycle one of the most enjoyable paths in Wales is the author's suggestion. This particularly attractive route is part of the former Ruabon to Barmouth railway. It survives as a footpath and cycleway and stretches between Dolgellau and Barmouth via Penmaenpool where the former signal box is now an RSPB visitor centre. There is also a wooden-constructed bridge crossing (toll) at this point which allows light traffic to cross the river and join the direct road to Barmouth, the A496. From Penmaenpool follow the path on foot or cycle for six miles and then, from the Morfa Mawddach station (on the Cambrian line) cross Barmouth Bridge and return by the same route. The views on this journey and especially from the bridge of the Mawddach valley and estuary are awe-inspiring but do not take the author's word for it! See it for oneself and reflect on the words of William Wordsworth who called it 'the sublime estuary… it could compare with the finest in Scotland'. The author is not sure what the Scots would make of that!

What to see locally: Harlech Castle (GPS: 52°51'40.35"N 4°6'37.43"W. OS: SH572311), a most imposing edifice, was built by Edward I in the late 13th century as one of his 'iron ring' of fortresses. Harlech, the most formidable, was designed to contain the Welsh in their mountains. However, in that respect it failed, for in 1404 it was taken by the Welsh rebel leader Owain Glyn Dŵr who proceeded to hold a parliament here. A long siege took place here during the Wars of the Roses and which it is believed was the inspiration of the stirring song *Men of Harlech*. Further along the line is Machynlleth, one time the capital of Wales and hence its continuing claim to be designated a 'city'. The town has much history but its main claim is as the location of the coronation of Owain Glyn Dŵr as the Prince of Wales in 1404. Glyn Dŵr also held his parliament in the town. There are several historic buildings including the Owain Glyn Dŵr Centre. Machynlleth is well known as the 'town with the clock' which is usually the first thing many visitors see when they arrive in the centre of Machynlleth. Built in the 1870s, it is the hub of the town from which the three main streets radiate. It is in need of repair and an appeal has been launched. Near Minffordd is the Italianate village of Portmeirion (GPS: 52°55'3.27"N 4°5'34.41"W) designed by Sir Bertram Clough Williams-Ellis and built between 1926 and 1939, and then again between 1954 and 1972. Apart from its pottery, the village is famous as the location for the filming of the 1960s cult TV series *The Prisoner*. The village is home to a tulip tree, a massive variegated sycamore and a weeping silver lime which scent the village in August. The gardens in and around village of Portmeirion have been cultivated since Victorian times with original specimen conifers, wellingtonia and Himalayan firs still remaining. (NB: Dogs are not allowed in the village.)

Neighbouring railways: Ffestiniog Railway, West Highland Railway, Welsh Highland Heritage Railway and the Talyllyn Railway. Arriva trains stop at the main line station at Minffordd.

Barmouth bridge on 6th August, 2009. This photograph was taken at low tide from Penrhyn Point looking up the beautiful Mawddach Valley. *Author*

25 Fairbourne Steam Railway

Location: Fairbourne.
GPS: Fairbourne: 52°41′51.22″N 4°3′5.32″W.
OS map reference: Fairbourne: SH615135.
Operator: Fairbourne Steam Railway.
Contact details: Fairbourne Steam Railway, Beach Road, Fairbourne, Gwynedd, LL38 2EX. Telephone: 01341 250362.
Route: Fairbourne village to Penrhyn Point (for the Barmouth Ferry) a distance of 2 miles.
Journey time: 20 minutes in each direction.
Gauge: Narrow (12¼ in.).
Website: www.fairbournerailway.com
Operating dates: Daily all year round (except between November and January although some Santa Specials are run). There are eight services per day in each direction.
History: The railway has being operated from Fairbourne village to Penrhyn Point since 1895. With the arrival of the Cambrian Coast Railway there were schemes to develop the area for tourism. As a consequence the tramway that had been used originally for transporting materials for constructing the village took on a new life as the Fairbourne Railway. Initially it had a 2 ft gauge but this was converted to 15 in. in 1916. The railway had mixed fortunes between World Wars I and II. The line closed in 1940 but was fortunately rescued by a group of Midlands' businessmen in 1946 and re-opened the following year. The line was redeveloped and new locomotives acquired. In the 1960s and early 1970s the railway enjoyed great success but people's holiday habits gradually changed in favour of 'going abroad' and so came a decline in the railway's popularity. The Ellerton family became the new owners in 1984. Two years later saw the adoption of the railway's third gauge, 12¼ in. With the exception of the diesel-powered *Sylvia* all the previous 15 in. gauge locomotives moved on. Four steam locomotives, half-size replicas of narrow gauge engines, were newly introduced. Two of these, one named *France* now renamed *Sherpa* and the other *Jubilee* now called *Yeo*, had previously run on the short-lived Réseau Guerlédan Railway in Brittany which had a very short life only operating between 1978 and 1979. The Fairbourne Railway, however, benefited from the demise of the Réseau Guerlédan by acquiring two locomotives which had never made it to France. On arrival at Fairbourne these two steam locomotives were named *Beddgelert* and *Russell*. The railway changed ownership in 1995 when Professor and Mrs Atkinson and Dr and Mrs Melton bought the line. They made significant investment both in the railway and the adjoining Rowen Nature Centre. In 2009, ownership of the railway transferred to a charitable body in order to ensure its long term future.
What to see locally: The Barmouth Bridge (OS: SH625155) can be well observed from Penrhyn Point or on the ferry which crosses the estuary of the Afon Mawddach from the railway's terminus to Barmouth. Rowen Nature Centre at Fairbourne is worth visiting. The coast road from Fairbourne to Tywyn offers superb views of the Lleyn Peninsula and Cardigan Bay. At a lower level these views are shared by the railway.
Neighbouring railways: Talyllyn Railway from Tywyn, 12 miles to the south.

Cader Idris as seen from Penrhyn Point. The Barmouth railway bridge can be seen centre stage with the Fairbourne train arriving close to its terminus at Penrhyn Point.   *Author*

Sherpa heads for Penrhyn Point on 7th August, 2009. The beaches here and at Barmouth are exquisite.   *Author*

26 Talyllyn Railway

Locations: Tywyn, Gwynedd and Abergynolwyn.
GPS: Tywyn: 52°35′9.37″N 4°5′34.23″W. Abergynolwyn: 52°38′41.14″N 3°57′12.75″W.
OS map references: Tywyn: SH636028. Abergynolwyn: SH681069.
Operator: Talyllyn Railway Company.
Contact details: Talyllyn Railway, Wharf Station, Tywyn, Gwynedd, LL36 9EY.
Telephone: 01654 710472. Fax: 01654 711755. E-mail: enquiries@talyllyn.co.uk
Route: Tywyn Wharf to Nant Gwernol via Pendre, Hendy Halt, Fach Goch Halt,
Cynfal Halt, Tynllwyn Halt, Rhydyronen, Brynglas, Dolgach Falls, Quarry
Siding Halt and Abergynolwyn, a distance of just over seven miles.
Journey time: 56 minutes.
Gauge: Narrow (2 ft 3 in.).
Traction and rolling stock: The two original steam locomotives and four
passenger coaches are still in regular use on the line together with others which
have been built or acquired over the years. Included are No. 1 *Talyllyn* built by
Fletcher Jennings in 1864, No. 2 *Dolgoch* also by Fletcher Jennings in 1866, No. 3
Sir Haydn by Hughes in 1878, No. 4 *Edward Thomas* by Kerr, Stuart in 1921, No.
6 *Douglas* by Barclay in 1918, and No. 7 *Tom Rolt* by the Talyllyn Railway in
1991. There are four diesel-powered locomotives and a variety of other traction.
There are 23 passenger carriages and brake vans and a selection of wagons.
Website: www.talyllyn.co.uk   This is a most impressive website published in
six languages! More details about the Narrow Gauge Railway Museum which
is also located at Tywyn Wharf station can be found at www.ngrm.org.uk and
in the next entry in this book.
Dolgoch Appeal: The Talyllyn Railway has recently made the following special
appeal. Locomotive No. 2 *Dolgoch* occupies a very special position in the history of
the Talyllyn Railway. It operated the first passenger trains in December 1866 and the
last services of the Haydn Jones era in October 1950. It also had the distinction of
working the first train of the railway preservation era on 14th May, 1951 and
continued, single-handed, working services for the remainder of that season.
Without *Dolgoch* the survival of the Talyllyn Railway would have been in serious
jeopardy. The locomotive was withdrawn at the end of the 1953 season and it was
10 years before it returned to Tywyn, fully rebuilt and with a new boiler. The boiler
is now at the end of its life and a new one will be required; it will be expensive with
estimates for the boiler being in the region of £60-70,000. Other work will also be
required on the chassis. The present boiler ticket expired in March 2010. It is hoped
that a successful appeal will allow *Dolgoch* to steam again for the sixtieth
anniversary (2011) of the first train in the UK railway preservation era, if not before.
Steam Railway magazine has made *Dolgoch* the subject of their specific appeal to their
readers, reflecting its unique place in railway preservation history. If readers of this
book would like to support this important appeal please visit the website:
www.talyllyn.co.uk/dolgoch-appeal and download the appeal form in pdf format.
Operating dates: Daily from April to October with additional services at
Christmas/New Year and during school half-term holidays. There are seven
services each way per day with one fewer in quieter periods during the
operating season.

Dolgoch hauls its train near to the Dolgoch Falls on 26th March, 2006. This locomotive, now out of service, must be preserved in working order (*see appeal on page 95*).

Author

Talyllyn pulling its train down towards Rhydyronen on 7th August, 2009.   *Author*

Dolgoch standing at Abergynolwyn station on 26th March, 2006.   *Author*

History: Originally opened in 1865 the narrow gauge line was built to carry slate from the quarries in the nearby hills. By 1909 the quarries had been closed by the then owner, W.H. McConnell. In 1911, the local MP, Sir Henry Haydn Jones, in the absence of finding a new buyer for the quarries, purchased them himself for the princely sum of £5,500. The quarries eventually closed in 1946 but the daily passenger train services continued for a while. At the beginning of the decade Sir Henry died and although his wife soldiered on, by October 1950 passenger services ended; however, good fortune was just around the corner. In 1951 responsibility for the railway was assumed by the Talyllyn Railway Preservation Society, thus providing continuity of services as well as earning the unique distinction as the first preserved heritage railway movement in the world, the grand-daddy of them all! Volunteer members of the society together with a small dedicated full-time workforce then and now continue to run the railway today. The Revd Wilfred Awdry was one of the first volunteer guards on the Talyllyn Railway and he was a vice-president of the Talyllyn Railway Preservation Society for many years (*see next entry*).

Railway constructions of interest: The viaduct near Dolgoch Falls.

What to see locally: The beautiful Tal-y-llyn (lake), further up the valley from Abergynolwyn, is superb with the convenience of the Tynycornel Hotel for refreshments. Aberdovey (w. *Aberdyfi* in common use locally) town, harbour and beach are well worth visiting An Outward Bound Sea School (which the author attended as a 16-year-old) operates out of the harbour. For the more energetic is a climb up Cader Idris, alt. 2,927 ft (900 m.) the ninth highest but the second most popular climbed mountain in Wales after Snowdon. *Cadair Idris* in Welsh means 'Arthur's chair'. Idris is believed to have been a 7th century warrior poet. It is said the mountain is haunted and that anyone who spends a night on the mountain will wake up either a madman or a poet - so be warned!

Neighbouring railways: Fairbourne Railway and the Corris Railway. Arriva trains pass through Tywyn *en route* from Barmouth to Machynlleth.

Comments: The promoting agency 'Great Little Trains of Wales' is based at the Wharf station in Tywyn where a discount card can be obtained for all 10 railways (*for details see page 22*). Tywyn is sometimes spelled Towyn. This railway's location is in Gwynedd and should not be confused with the Towyn near Rhyl and the Towyn near Cardigan in Ceredigion. There is also a Tywyn near Deganwy not far from Llandudno. All the Tywyn/Towyns are long distances apart! NB: The GPS and OS map references.

27 The Narrow Gauge Railway Museum

Location: Tywyn.
GPS: Tywyn: 52°35'9.37"N 4°5'34.23"W.
OS map reference: Tywyn: SH636028.
Contact details: The Narrow Gauge Museum, Wharf Station, Tywyn, Gwynedd, LL36 9EY. Telephone: 01654 710472. E-mail: curator@ngrm.org.uk
Gauge: 'Narrow' is defined as anything less than the standard gauge of 4 ft 8½ in.

What can be seen: Many railways in England, Ireland and Wales are represented by a wide variety of exhibits. Visitors can discover the role played in the development of the communities of Tywyn and the Fathew valley with the quarrying of slate, and its transportation out by the Talyllyn Railway. One can contrast this with the experience of other narrow gauge railways in the UK in accessing other areas of the countryside, some very remote, and in supporting industries such as mining, manufacturing, forestry, agriculture and tourism. Of course such railways were not restricted just to rural areas. Town and cities with their industries also benefited as did military establishments for the movement of ordnance as well as in support of troops on the battlefields. On the ground floor of the museum the story is told of the historical development of narrow gauge, permanent way, industrial, military and slate railways. The displays include a 3 ft 6 in. gauge wooden wagon from the Forest of Dean, which was horse-drawn and dates back to about the turn of the 19th century. Other important exhibits are *George Henry, Rough Pup* and *Jubilee 1897,* all typical slate quarry locomotives but all differing in their design for the work. A Dundee Gasworks locomotive and the unique Guinness Brewery locomotive with its motion on top of the boiler illustrate the ingenuity and diversity of narrow gauge railways in industry. Narrow gauge railways as 'public carriers' are featured on the first floor, along with an interesting section on signalling. A balcony allows visitors a view of the Wharf station site and the Cambrian Coast railway line passing nearby.

Website: www.ngrm.org.uk

Operating dates: Open daily from the beginning of April to the end of October, usually 1000 to 1400 hours. The museum is closed for the whole of January and to early February but thereafter it is open at some weekends until the end of March. It is wise to check opening times/dates on the website or by telephone beforehand. Entrance is free but donations are always much appreciated.

History: The Narrow Gauge Railway Museum began life in the 1950s when the Talyllyn Railway Preservation Society was established to operate the Talyllyn Railway (*see entry 26*). In 1964, a charitable trust was formed to manage and develop the museum, a responsibility assumed in 1994 by the present Narrow Gauge Railway Museum Trust. The original museum building dating from the 1950s was, in spite of an extension in 1964, found towards the end of the century to have significant limitations. About the same time the railway was looking to improve its station facilities. Consequently, in 2000 an appeal was launched to raise funds to build a new station and a museum on the Tywyn Wharf site. Success of the appeal, with added help from the Heritage Lottery Fund, raised sufficient funds to allow for the construction of a two-storey building to house the museum. Construction work began in 2001 leading to the new station and museum complex being opened by HRH The Prince of Wales in July 2005. The Revd Wilfred Awdry of *Thomas the Tank Engine* fame was one of the first volunteer guards and was a vice-president of the Talyllyn Railway Preservation Society for many years. As a matter of interest the Talyllyn Railway's locomotives all appeared in the Thomas books as alter-ego characters, and many of the stories written have evolved from real-life tales of the Talyllyn in its early years. There is a section in the museum devoted to Awdry and his work and comprises a replica of his study where he wrote his books; it is authentic in that many of his personal

Talyllyn Railway's No. 3 being given a final polish before its departure on 17th April, 2010. In the background is the station building with the museum at the far end. On the second floor of the museum is a balcony overlooking the yard.   *Author*

The replica of the Revd Awdry's study in the Narrow Gauge Railway Museum.   *Author*

The signalling display in the Narrow Gauge Railway Museum at Tywyn. *Author*

belongings, books and office equipment are on display. The 'study' is normally locked but can be viewed through a window. The author, however, was privileged to be given access, noticing on entering the odour of tobacco smoke in the air. It seems that Revd Awdry was an enthusiastic pipe smoker, the residue of which has impregnated the books, furniture and equipment to this day!

What to see locally: At Abergynolwyn, about six miles north-east of Tywyn, is the remains of Castell-y-Bere, a native Welsh castle, probably begun by Prince Llywelyn ab Iorwerth (the Great) around 1221. The castle featured in yet another 13th century conflict between the Welsh and the English. In the war of 1282-83 it was besieged by an English army from Montgomery under Edward I's lieutenant, the Savoyard Sir Otto de Grandison.

What to do locally: On the railway in August each year there is a 'Race the Train' event run over five different courses each offering various distances and standards of running ability, including a toddlers run. Many charities invariably benefit from this event.

What to remember locally: Tywyn, which in English means 'seashore', 'sand-dune' or 'beach' was a major training ground for the amphibious warfare landings in World War II and a strategic war base was also located here. Defences in the form of 'pillboxes' can still be seen on the coastline to the south of the town. In 1914, the Marconi Company built a long wave receiver station in Tywyn operating in conjunction with a high-power transmitter station at Waunfawr near Llanrug in Snowdonia. In 1921, the Tywyn and Waunfawr stations initiated a transatlantic wireless telegraph service with a similar wireless transmitting and receiving stations in New Jersey in the United States of America belonging to the Radio Corporation of America (RCA). This transatlantic service eventually replaced Marconi's transatlantic telegraph station at Clifden in Ireland which had been destroyed in 1922 during the Irish Civil War.

Neighbouring railways: Arriva's Cambrian line from Porthmadog to Machynlleth via Barmouth and, of course, the Talyllyn Railway itself.

Comments: The museum is well worth visiting especially by those interested in industrial heritage. As noted elsewhere, Tywyn is sometimes spelled Towyn and should not be confused with the other Tywyn/Towyns.

'Tattoo' class No. 7 pushes its gaily-painted carriages towards Corris station on 8th August, 2009.   *Author*

28 Corris Railway

Location: Corris.
GPS: Corris: 52°39'4.23"N 3°50'36.60"W.
OS map reference: Corris: SH755075.
Operator: Corris Railway.
Contact details: Corris Railway, Station Yard, Corris, Machynlleth, SY20 9SH.
Telephone: 01654 761303. Email: enquiries@corris.co.uk
Route: Corris station to the engine shed at Maespoeth, where there is a short tour, and then return to Corris station. Single journeys cannot be taken at present owing to planning stipulations.
Journey time: Round trip takes about 50 minutes.
Gauge: Narrow (2 ft 3 in.).
Traction: The construction of a new steam locomotive, a 'Tattoo' class, No. 7, was completed and delivered to the Corris railway on 17th May, 2005. It is a modern version of a Kerr, Stuart locomotive and is similar to No. 4 *Edward Thomas* on the neighbouring Talyllyn Railway. No. 7, in keeping with the Corris tradition, does not carry a name.
Website: www.corris.co.uk
Operating dates: April to September at weekends and additionally on Mondays and Tuesdays at the end of July and in August. Services also operate on Bank Holidays, Easter and one weekend before Christmas. Trains normally leave Corris on the hour between 1100 and 1600 hours.
History: Towards the end of 1966 some East Midlands members of the nearby Talyllyn Railway Preservation Society formed the Corris Railway Society. They had four objectives; viz. to preserve what remained of the Corris line; to research its history; to open a museum to display artefacts and photographs; and, to examine the feasibility of re-opening part of the original route to passengers. By 1970, the Corris Railway Museum had been opened in some buildings remaining at Corris station. In 1971, a 'demonstration track' was laid at the south end of the station yard, adjacent to the museum, but officialdom at that time prevented it from travelling more than a few hundred yards. In 1981, the Maespoeth engine shed and yard was handed over to the railway by the Forestry Commission. Official approval for the reinstatement of the track between Corris and Maespoeth was achieved in 1984 and the following year saw the 'First Train back to Corris'. Steam-driven traction returned to the line in 1996 but passengers were not allowed to be carried until the summer of 2002. In the summer of the following year the railway staged a grand re-opening ceremony with the assistance of the Talyllyn Railway. The latter have continued to provide invaluable help to this developing heritage railway.
Railway constructions of interest: The 1878-built engine shed at Maespoeth.
What to see locally: The spectacular caverns and the great waterfall of King Arthur's Labyrinth and Bard's Quest which is near to Corris station and can be accessed from the Corris Craft Centre on the main A487.
What to know locally: Corris lies on the west bank of the Afon (river) Dulas and derives its names from the English word 'quarries' given the extensive slate industry that surrounded the village. The Dulas defines the boundary beween the

Arriva's dmu No. 158824 approaching Dovey Junction from Machynlleth on 8th August, 2009.
Author

Dovey Junction's recently completed extra long platforms. Whilst there is no community to serve here the junction station allows passengers to transfer between trains to and from Aberystwyth and those to Barmouth without travelling into Machynlleth. The track to the left is for Aberystwyth and to the right for Aberdovey, Barmouth and beyond. *Author*

current counties of Gwynedd and Powys, formerly Merioneth and Montgomery. The village is on the edge of the Snowdonia National Park but not within it.
Neighbouring railways: Talyllyn Railway.
Comments: The railway is billed as 'In the Heart of the Land of the Little Trains'. There is an interesting railway museum at Corris station which is open only on days when passenger services are operating.

29 Cambrian Lines - Machynlleth to Aberystwyth

Locations: Machynlleth and Aberystwyth.
GPS: Machynlleth: 52°35'30.97"N 3°51'9.89"W. Aberystwyth: 52°24'58.03"N 4°5'1.67"W.
OS map references: Machynlleth SH748012. Aberystwyth: SN585815.
Operator: Arriva Trains Wales.
Timetable: Arriva No. 1.
Route: Machynlleth to Aberystwyth via Dovey Junction and Borth.
Journey time: 27 minutes.
Website: www.arrivatrainswales.co.uk
Operating dates: Daily with services every two hours.
Railway constructions of interest: The modern station, or really platforms, at Dovey Junction is amazing in that it offers two platforms, one of which is very long, and which with its small shelter, is located in the middle of nowhere! The prime reason that it is there to allow passengers on the separate Barmouth and Aberystwyth routes to change trains when it not possible to do so further up the line at nearby Machynlleth. Bird watchers, however, can benefit from this location (*see next section*).
What to see locally: On reaching the summit of Constitution Hill in Aberystwyth, on foot or by using the cliff railway, one has a superb view which, weather permitting, extends from the Preseli Hills of Pembrokeshire in the south, the expanse of Cardigan Bay to the west and to Snowdonia in the north. As many as 26 mountain peaks can be seen from here on clear day. At the summit there is a café and the famous Camera Obscura. The original Camera Obscura was opened in the castle grounds at the other end of the promenade in 1880 but by 1920s it had gone as entertainment tastes changed. The present building, completed in 1985, is fitted with a 14 inch lens making it the world's largest camera obscura. A precision balanced mirror revolves taking detailed views of the surrounding countryside which are thrown onto a viewing table in the centre of the building. It is said that it is possible to view up to an amazing 1,000 squares mile with outstanding clarity. Aberystwyth has a 12/13th century castle, now ruined, perched on a hilltop above the town which was built by Llywelyn ab Iorwerth. For those interested in bird-watching there is much to offer. Not far away is RSPB's Ynyslas National Nature Reserve on the Dyfi estuary. Further up from Ynyslas is Cors Dyfi Nature Reserve, off the A487 and just over three miles south-west of Machynlleth; it is the site of the exciting Dyfi Osprey project. Incidentally, Dovey Junction station platform (which can only be accessed by a mile walk on foot from the A487) is an ideal vantage point for viewing the nest, with the benefit of powerful binoculars or a spotting scope, of course.

Steam locomotive *Prince of Wales* heading five distinctively-liveried passenger carriages approaches Capel Bangor, where, at the station, there is a passing loop. Photographed on 8th August, 2009.   *Author*

No. 8 leaving Aberystwyth on a very wet summer's day in July 2009.   *Author*

Neighbouring railways: The Aberystwyth Electric Cliff Railway, opened in 1896, is the longest electric cliff railway in Britain. On first opening it operated by means of a water balance system but in 1921 it was converted to run on electric power. It climbs Constitution Hill from the northern end of the town's promenade. 'Trains' run every few minutes on the cliff railway from mid-March to early November.

Comments: Aberystwyth is a university town with a student population of 7,000 students. Their liquid refreshment is apparently well catered for as it is said there are about 50 public houses in the town! Aberystwyth is the home of the National Library of Wales.

30 Vale of Rheidol Railway

Locations: Aberystwyth and Devil's Bridge:
GPS: Aberystwyth: 52°24'58.03"N 4°5'1.67"W. Devil's Bridge: 52°22'31.76"N 3°51'23.63"W.
OS map references: Aberystwyth: SN585815. Devil's Bridge: SN643749.
Operator: Vale of Rheidol Railway.
Contact details: Vale of Rheidol Railway, Park Avenue, Aberystwyth, Cardiganshire, SY23 1PG. Telephone: 01970 625819. Fax: 01970 623769. Email: vor@rheidolrailway.co.uk
Route: Aberystwyth to Devil's Bridge via Capel Bangor station which is also a passing loop, Nantyronen (where there is a water tank facility), Aberffwd (another passing loop), a total distance of almost 12 miles.
Journey time: One hour each way.
Gauge: Narrow (1 ft 11¾ in.).
Traction: The locomotives and carriages currently in use were built for the line by the Great Western Railway between 1923 and 1938.
Website: www.rheidolrailway.co.uk
Operating dates: Daily from early April to the end of October with two services each way each day and four on peak days in summer.
History: The construction of the Vale of Rheidol Light Railway was authorized by Act of Parliament in 1897. At that time it was the most up-to-date in narrow gauge railway construction. The railway was routed through challenging terrain where it would have been impossible to build a standard gauge line without incurring prohibitive costs. Following some delay, not least financial, the railway was opened to the general public at the end of 1902. It was hoped that the building of the railway would bring prosperity back to some of the local lead mines in the area and some did re-open. The movement of timber was profitable especially of pit props for the developing coal mines in South Wales. In 1912, consideration was given to converting the line to electric traction, using hydro-electric power from the River Rheidol. However, in the same year, control of the line passed to the Cambrian Railways who shelved the plans. World War I saw a reduction in passenger services, and later a decline in freight traffic. In 1923, Cambrian Railways were taken over by the Great Western Railway which saw freight movement completely withdrawn and the harbour branch of the line closed. The winter passenger

A train hauled by the steam locomotive *Prince of Wales* having just left Capel Bangor steams towards Devil's Bridge on 8th August, 2009.   *Caroline Jones*

services were withdrawn in 1930 and later the line was closed for the duration of the World War II. In 1948, British Railways took over the railway and, perhaps surprisingly, it survived the Beeching cuts. As a consequence it earned the distinction of being the last British Rail(ways)-owned steam railway. In 1989, the railway was privatized and is now owned by a charitable trust.

Railway constructions of interest: If one stands close to the visitor centre at Rheidol power station one can admire the feat of engineering in building this line which clings desperately to the steep sides of the hill above the river.

What to see locally: The three bridges at Devil's Bridge and the waterfalls are well worth a visit. For the active, there is a walk to enjoy on the nearby 45 minute nature trail. It is possible to take this walk between trains but there is no time to linger as the train departs for Aberystwyth an hour after its arrival. However, travellers can make the return journey on any train, subject to availability, thus making for a more leisurely walk. For those who travel by car, on the opposite bank of the river to the railway, is the Rheidol power station operated by the Norwegian company, Statkraft Energy. Extending over 160 km^2, it is the largest hydro-electric scheme in England and Wales. The Afon Rheidol leaves the reservoir at Nant-y-moch in the shadow of the Pumlumon mountains and runs south towards Ponterwyd and continues down to Devil's Bridge from where it heads west down the Rheidol valley to Aberystwyth draining into Cardigan Bay. There is a visitor centre near the Rheidol Falls to appreciate. Guided tours of the power station and its nearby fish farm are offered as well as a local nature trail to follow. The valley is full of interest including the former lead and iron mine workings. Bird watchers benefit again in this area for nine miles east of Aberystwyth on the A44 at Bwlch Nant yr Arian (GPS: 52°24′39.36″N 3°52′12.23″W), near the village of Ponterwyd, is the Welsh Forestry Commission's Visitor Centre. Red kite gather here before feeding time, i.e. 1400 hours in winter and 1500 hours in summer. It is a truly an amazing sight to see these rare birds of prey congregating about an hour before the feed is laid and then observe them take their profit on the wing. Bwlch yr Nant Forestry Commission site (OS: SN718813) is five miles north-east of Devil's Bridge.

Neighbouring railway: Cambrian lines with Arriva services from Aberystwyth to Machynlleth and Aberdovey to Machynlleth.

31 Cambrian Lines - Machynlleth to Welshpool for Shrewsbury

Locations: Machynlleth and Welshpool for Shrewsbury.
GPS: Machynlleth: 52°35′30.97″N 3°51′9.89″W. Welshpool: 52°39′34.58″N 3° 8′50.00″W. Shrewsbury 52°42′2.48″N 2°45′23.44″W.
OS map references: Machynlleth SH748012. Welshpool: SJ225075. Shrewsbury: SJ492124.
Operator: Arriva Trains Wales.
Timetable: Arriva No. 1.
Route: Machynlleth to Welshpool via Newtown and Caersws, a distance of 38 miles.
Journey time: 54 minutes.
Website: www.arrivatrainswales.co.uk
Operating dates: Daily with services every two hours.
Railway constructions of interest: The interesting old station at Welshpool is now converted to a shopping emporium.
What to see locally: Welshpool livestock market is the largest one day market of livestock in Wales and one of the largest centres for sales of prime and breeding sheep in Europe. Sales are held every Monday.
Neighbouring railways: Vale of Rheidol at one end and the Welshpool & Llanfair Light Railway at the other.
Comments: The Carno Station Action Group was set up in 2002 as a sub-committee of the local Community Council to campaign for the opening of Carno railway station on the Cambrian Line between Shrewsbury and Aberystwyth. Carno is a growing village with a population of about 750 and is likely to grow further with the redevelopment of the former Laura Ashley factory site now closed. Carno is located on the longest stretch of railway in the whole of Wales (22 miles) without an intermediate station. Carno is six miles from Caersws and 16 miles from Machynlleth.

An Arriva morning train on 15th January, 2010 heads for Welshpool, seen near Abermule running alongside the main A483 road. Near here in January 1921 there was head-on collision between two trains caused by a misunderstanding between staff which compromised the safety apparatus - Tyer's Electric Train Tablet. A total of 17 passengers were killed and 36 injured. Lord Herbert Vane-Tempest, a Director of the Cambrian Railways, was killed in the accident. *Author*

An Arriva service crosses the near-frozen Afon Carno near Caersws on 15th January, 2010.
Author

The modern Welshpool station as photographed on 17th April, 2010. The old station building, now a shopping emporium, is in the background. The old station's platform still exists but the former trackbed in front of it is now part of the town bypass.   *Author*

32 Welshpool & Llanfair Light Railway (WLLR)

Locations: Welshpool and Llanfair Caereinion.
GPS: Welshpool: 52°39'34.58"N 3°8'50.00"W. Llanfair Caereinion: 52°38'53.50"N 3°19'33.08"W.
OS map references: Welshpool: SJ225075. Llanfair Caereinion: SJ105065.
Operator: Welshpool & Llanfair Light Railway.
Contact details: Welshpool & Llanfair Light Railway, The Station, Llanfair Caereinion, Powys, SY21 0SF. Telephone: 01938 810441. Fax: 01938 810861.
Route: Welshpool (Raven Square) to Llanfair Caereinion via Sylfaen, Castle Caereinion, Cyfronydd, and Heniarth, a distance of eight miles.
Journey time: 50 minutes.
Gauge: Narrow (2 ft 6 in.).
Traction: Services are always provided by steam traction which includes No. 1/822 *The Earl*, No. 2/823 *Countess*, No. 12 *Joan*, and No. 19/764-425. No 8. *Dougal* may be used at special events. No. 14/85 will be out of service from April 2010 for an indefinite period awaiting a major overhaul as are No. 10/699.01 and 18/764-823. No. 6 *Monarch* may be seen on static display. There are some diesels for permanent way work etc.
Rolling Stock: Carriages are from Austria, Hungary, and Sierra Leone, and there are replicas of two of the original W&LLR carriages which are due to be joined by a third in August 2010. Goods vehicles permit the operation of mixed trains and demonstration freight trains.
Website: www.wllr.org.uk
Operating dates: Weekends from Easter to October. Services also operate on other days of the week, which vary according to the time of year, and are daily from mid-July to early September. There is an annual steam gala in September and Santa Specials are run during the last two weekends before Christmas. See the website or printed timetable for details of services and special events.
History: The railway was built to connect the local farming communities with the local market town of Welshpool. It was first operated by the Cambrian Railways until it was taken over first by the Great Western Railway and later, in 1948, by British Railways as part of the nationalization programme. After 1931, the railway only moved freight but this came to an end in 1956 long before Dr Beeching had come onto the railway scene. As is so often the case with heritage railways, a group of enthusiasts banded together to take over the line with the objective of opening it to tourist traffic. Moves for take over initially started in 1952, before the line had closed, but things were not straightforward, and the first passenger-carrying trains did not run until late 1962, with a proper timetabled service starting in 1963. The product of the enthusiasts' labours is what the visitor can acknowledge and enjoy today.
Railway constructions of interest: Brynelin viaduct near Cyfronydd station, and the Banwy bridge near Heniarth station where are also some steep gradients and tight curves to appreciate.
What to see locally: In 2009/10 the Welshpool Smithfield livestock market has been relocated to a new purpose-built site and is an interesting spectacle to see on Mondays every week. The former site, closer to the town centre is being

No. 14/85, formerly used in the Sierra Leone, was photographed near Cyfronydd as it leads its train towards Llanfair Caereinion on 16th July, 2005. The boiler certificate on this locomotive expired on Saturday 17th April, 2010 and is now out of service for the foreseeable future.

Author

No. 2/823 *Countess* leaves Castell Caereinion station on 17th April, 2010. *Author*

No. 2/823 *Countess* arrives at the Raven Square station at Welshpool on 17th April, 2010.

Author

No. 8 *Dougal* (the diminutive Barclay) was photographed at Llanfair Caereinion on 16th July, 2005.

Author

A midday Arriva service heading for Shrewsbury crosses the *circa* 1865-built Knucklas viaduct on a snowy 19th February, 2010. *Caroline Jones*

An Arriva morning train heading for Shrewsbury crosses the Cynghordy viaduct on 26th February, 2010. It is said that the pillars are as deep below the ground as they are above. A local resident reported that as the viaduct was being completed in 1867 a worker fell into the hollow pillar, his body remaining there ever since. *Author*

redeveloped for retail use. In the town there is a six-sided, brick-built cockpit which was constructed in the early 18th century. It was in regular use for cockfighting until the barbaric practice was outlawed in 1849. This is the only unaltered cockpit preserved on its original site in Great Britain. Nearby is the Montgomery Canal, known colloquially as 'The Monty'. Originally planned only to run from Llanymynech through Welshpool to Newtown, the canal now travels a longer 33 miles from Frankton Junction on the Llangollen Canal. The canal fell into disuse following a breach in 1936, and was eventually abandoned in 1944. However, with recent growth in interest in canals for leisure purposes, restoration projects have achieved the navigable use of seven miles on the northern section, from Frankton Junction to Gronwen Wharf, a short stretch at Llanymynech, and a central section of the canal around Welshpool. Restoration work continues but in the meantime the canal towpath offers excellent walking in most attractive countryside. There are also a number of attractive walks around the W&LLR route for which a booklet has been produced and is available locally.

Neighbouring railways: Cambrian Heritage Railways. Arriva trains operate on the Cambrian Line from Machynlleth to Shrewsbury passing through the modern station at Welshpool.

33 Heart of Wales Line

Locations: Shrewsbury and Swansea.
GPS: Shrewsbury: 52°42′2.48″N 2°45′23.44″W. Swansea: 51°37′13.59″N 3°56′47.86″W.
OS map references: Shrewsbury: SJ492124. Swansea: SS657938.
Operator: Arriva Trains Wales.
Timetable: Arriva No. 1.
Route: Shrewsbury (in England) to Swansea via Church Stretton, Craven Arms, Broome, Hopton Heath, Bucknell, and into Wales at Knighton, then Knucklas, Llangynllo, Llanbister Road, Dolau, Pen-y-Bont, Llandrindod, Builth Road, Cilmeri, Garth (Powys), Llangammarch, Llanwrtyd, Sugar Loaf, Cynghordy, Llandovery, Llawrda, Llangadog, Llandeilo, Ffairfach, Llandybie, Ammanford, Pantyffynnon, Ponterddulais, Llangennech, Bynea, Llanelli, Gowerton and Swansea, a distance of about 125 miles.
Journey time: 3 hours 52 minutes.
Website: www.arrivatrainswales.co.uk Another interesting and useful website is www.heartofwales.co.uk
Operating dates: Daily (except Sundays), but infrequent, with only four services in each direction.
Railway constructions of interest: The 18-arch 1867-built Cynghordy viaduct (GPS: 52°2′30.17″N 3°44′15.50″W. OS: SN807417) five miles north-east of Llandovery built in 1867, the Knucklas viaduct (GPS: 52°21′37.23″N 3°6′7.49″W SO251741) built *circa* 1865 and the Sugar Loaf tunnel (1,001 yards long). Near to Pantyffynnon station, three miles south of Ammanford, there is a century-old GWR signal box which controls all the signalling for the line until it reaches as

far as Craven Arms. The Glanrhyd Bridge, over the River Towy near Llandeilo, has a sad history. On 19th October, 1987, four people died when an early morning train passenger train, a two-car class '108' dmu *en route* from Swansea to Shrewsbury, fell into the river after the Glanrhyd bridge collapsed under the train following flooding.

What to see locally: Gigrin Farm (GPS: 52°17'48.48"N 3°29'39.42"W) on South Street, Rhayader (OS: SN980677) is a family-run sheep farm situated in outstandingly beautiful countryside with views of the Wye and Elan valleys. Gigrin Farm became an official Red Kite Feeding Station at the request of the RSPB in 1992/93. At that time there were six red kites roosting locally but by the winter of 2006 over 400 were coming in daily to feed. Not only can the red kite be seen at the farm but also the black kite and the rare white kite, the correct term for the latter being the 'leucistic'. The BBC Wildlife Magazine described Gigrin Farm as 'Surely the largest, most fantastic bird table in the world'. Never have been truer words stated. A visit to the farm, where visitors are always made most welcome to view the spectacle from purpose-built hides, is most worthwhile. Gigrin Farm is about 10 miles north-west of Llandrindod Wells. The website at www.gigrin.co.uk is also well worth viewing preparatory to a visit.

Neighbouring railways: The Llangollen Railway and Cambrian Heritage Railways in the north and Llanelli & MMR, Gwili and Teifi Railways in the south.

Passengers on this Arriva service in the summer of 2009 enjoy the beautiful scenery as the train approaches Llandeilo having not long crossed the River Towy near Pont Gwladys.
Author

34 Gwili Railway (and Swansea Vale Railway)

Location: Bronwydd Arms off the A484 three miles north of Carmarthen.
GPS: Bronwydd Arms: 51°53'50.43"N 4°18'3.88"W.
OS map reference: Bronwydd Arms: SN415245.
Operator: Gwili Steam Railway.
Contact details: Gwili Steam Railway, Bronwydd Arms Station, Carmarthen, SA33 6HT. Telephone: 01267 238213
Route: Bronwydd Arms to Danycoed Halt, near Cynwyl Elfed (GPS: 51°55'20.19"N 4°22'1.77"W), a distance of just over three miles and running close to the River Gwili all of the way. The route was originally part of the Carmarthen to Aberystwyth line, which must have been a magnificent journey in its day. The line passes through Llwyfan Cerrig where a miniature railway is located with a picnic site nearby.
Journey time: 15 minutes each way.
Gauge: The only standard gauge heritage steam railway operating in West Wales.
Steam traction: 1944-built Robert Stephenson & Hawthorn 0-6-0 saddle tank No. 71516 *Welsh Guardsman*, 1914-built Avonside Engine Company colliery engine *Sir John*, 1945-built Andrew Barclay 0-4-0 saddle tank *Victory*, the austerity locomotive *Haulwen* and a 1942-built Robert Stephenson & Hawthorn 0-4-0 saddle tank *Olwen*. There are two former Swansea Vale Railway (*see below*) locomotives, a 1955-built Hunslet austerity locomotive and a Peckett *Mond Nickel No. 1*.
Diesel traction: Includes BR class '117' 3-car dmu Nos. 51347/59508/51401, D2178 British Rail '03' class shunter, two North British Locomotive Company shunting engines built for British Steel and two Ruston & Hornsby industrial engines.
Other rolling stock: The Gwili Railway has a fine collection of vintage coaches including a Taff Vale Railway (TVR) coach No. 145 built in 1874 and which is the oldest standard gauge coach surviving a Welsh railway company, TVR No. 220 built 1891 and sometimes used for passenger trains and GWR No. 216 built in 1888 and in the process of being restored. There are two other 19th century coaches awaiting restoration.
Website: www.gwili-railway.co.uk
Operating dates: April to October mainly at weekends and school holidays with four services daily each way. However, a fuller programme of daily trains with five services each way operates from the last week of July to the end of August. Christmas Santa Specials as well as other events are also offered throughout the operating season. See the website for more detail. Steam driving experience days are available throughout the year but book in advance as places are limited.
Tariff: Pay once and ride all day.
History of the line: A broad-gauge railway was originally opened in 1860 by the then South Wales Railway which a year later became Carmarthen & Cardigan Railway Company. The first section of line ran from Carmarthen to Conwil (w. *Cynwyl*) with the intention in time of the line connecting with Cardigan. It never

Haulwen is photographed passing under the bridge at Pentre Morgan as she heads back to Bronwydd Arms on 11th July, 2009. *Author*

Originally built in 1945 by the Vulcan Foundry, this austerity locomotive named *Haulwen* was rebuilt in 1961 by Hunslet. She is photographed here not far from the cricket ground as she heads back to Bronwydd Arms on 11th July, 2009. *Author*

did. Indeed it only managed to reach Newcastle Emlyn by 1895. In 1872, the line had become the last in Wales to be converted from Brunel's broad gauge to standard gauge. A separate connection was made by the Manchester & Milford Railway Company from Aberystwyth via Lampeter to a junction with the Carmarthen line at Pencader, thus establishing an important North-South Wales connection. In its early days, the line was active serving the farming and woollen industries but after World Wars I and II traffic steadily declined. First branches off the main line closed and by the mid-1960s under the Beeching cuts most had gone. The last service ran in 1973 and two years later the track was lifted. The Gwili Railway Company was established in the same year to preserve the eight mile route from Abergwili Junction to Llanpumpsaint. By 1978 it had managed to rescue a mile of track and the first train ran, a Peckett steam locomotive 0-4-0 named *Merlin* hauling a single coach. This distinguished the Gwili as the first standard-gauge preserved railway to operate in Wales. Since those days the railway has expanded to Danycoed where a station was opened in 2001. There are plans to extend the railway south to the outskirts of Carmarthen to a new terminus at the old Abergwili Junction, about one mile of track has already been laid. An important part of this development has been the arrival of the members and their resources from the Swansea Vale Railway.

Swansea Vale Railway: The original Swansea Vale Railway located in the Lower Swansea Valley goes back to the days of the industrial revolution when, in 1816, Scott's tram road was constructed to transport coal from Scott's Pit, near Birchgrove, four miles to the south to the wharves on the River Tawe. (Incidentally it is believed that the engine house of Scott's Pit can still be seen close to the M4 motorway between junctions 44 and 45.) In 1845, the Swansea Vale Railway Company was formed to rebuild the line as a modern standard gauge railway. By agreement with the then broad gauge South Wales Railway a junction of the two lines was made at Six Pit. To be successful this required the line from Six Pit to Swansea harbour to be dual gauged. Being keen to link up with Swansea Docks the Midland Railway purchased the line in 1876 creating the link they wanted with the benefit of the Neath & Brecon Railway. The railway was successful for many years but by 1922 a decline had begun. Reduced services and closures followed so that by 1985 all that remained was the line preserved by the Swansea Vale Railway Society (SVR) on leases granted by Swansea City Council. Despite some problems, vandalism for example, some progress was made including running a few services. Unfortunately, the end came when a decision was made by Swansea City Council in 2005 not to renew the leases. There followed much heartache followed by protracted negotiations with the Swansea City Council but eventually a conclusion was reached when some grant funding was made available to facilitate the move. The Gwili Railway at Bronwydd Arms had offered a home to the SVR which, as it turns out, is fortuitous for both railways with the SVR being able to bring significant resources which will eventually aid the Gwili's extension south to Carmarthen. Locomotives, rolling stock, a signal box, signals, a footbridge, plant and tools etc have already been moved or are about to be. After much disappointment the future looks bright.

Railway constructions of interest: The signal box at Bronwydd Arms came from Llandybie. The halt at Danycoed has been built in traditional GWR style.

The signal box here at Bronwydd Arms was sourced from Llandybie, near Ammanford.

Author

The station building at Llwyfan Cerrig, opened in 1988, came from Felin Fach on the Aberaeron line; it was taken down plank by plank by volunteers and rebuilt on this site.

What to see locally: Gwili Pottery, nearby at Pontarsais, produces beautiful hand-thrown, hand-painted, earthenware ceramics in both traditional and contemporary designs.

Neighbouring railways: Arriva services run on the West Wales line to Carmarthen and beyond. The Teifi Valley Railway is a narrow gauge tourist line operating on part of the same original route (*see next entry*).

Comments: The railway has been running for over 30 years supported by an active Gwili Railway Preservation Society. The railway has starred in various television dramas including *Carrie's War* and *The Edge of Love*. Andrew Marr, the television presenter, visited the railway when filming for the recent series *The Making of Modern Britain*. Mr Marr reported on the Taff Vale Railway strike of 1901 when the railway company successfully sued the Amalgamated Society of Railway Servants for damages. Photographic charters catering specifically for rail enthusiasts are held from time to time. There is a café facility in an old railway coach at Bronwydd Arms.

The marshalling yard at Bronwydd Arms with *Haulwen* manoeuvring on 11th July, 2009.
Author

Boys of all ages love their trains! *Alan George* steams out of its shed on 1st August, 2009.

Author

35 Teifi Valley Railway

Location: Henllan, near Newcastle Emlyn.
GPS: Henllan: 52°3'17.47"N 4°24'36.25"W.
OS map reference: Henllan: SN355405.
Operator: Teifi Valley Railway.
Contact details: Teifi Valley Railway, Henllan Station, Newcastle Emlyn, SA44 5TD. Telephone: 01559 371077.
Route: Henllan to Llandyfriog Riverside with request stops at Pontprenshitw and Forest Halt, a total distance of about two miles.
Journey time: 40 minutes round trip.
Gauge: Narrow (2 ft).
Traction: Originally from Penrhyn Quarry in North Wales (*see entry 14*) is the steam locomotive *Alan George* which is 115 years old and still working hard. There is also a World War I locomotive, *Sgt. Murphy*, which was intended for duties in France but never made it. It eventually arrived on the Ffestiniog Railway where it was rebuilt and later came to this railway. Also safeguarded is a 'Joffre' class steam locomotive, also a veteran of World War I and a predecessor of *Sgt. Murphy*, which it is hoped soon to restore. There is also some diesel traction.
Website: www.teifivalleyrailway.com
Operating dates: From Easter to the end of October with special trains at Christmas.
Tariff: Pay once and ride all day.
History: The original broad gauge line was intended to transport passengers and freight from Carmarthen to Cardigan via Newcastle Emlyn and Llandysul. In 1854, an Act of Parliament allowed for the purchase of lands from Carmarthen to Newcastle Emlyn to allow for the construction of the railway. In 1860, the first section of line was opened from Carmarthen to Conwil, at that time services being operated briefly by the then South Wales Railway. A year later this railway came under the ownership of the Carmarthen & Cardigan Railway. Extensions of the line to Pencader and then Llandysul were completed in 1864. From the latter, a horse-drawn bus could be taken to complete the rest of the journey to Cardigan. In 1872, the line was converted to standard gauge although parts had already been modified to mixed gauge. The railway company, by the time it reached Llandysul, suffered financial difficulties and became insolvent. It was soon realised that Cardigan was not going to be reached. The development of the line was hindered in particular by the difficulties presented by the location of the Cenarth Falls on the River Teifi. The falls had become a popular tourist attraction with easy access from the road running through the gorge. Unfortunately, there was insufficient room in the gorge to accommodate both a railway and a road. The Great Western Railway purchased the railway in 1881 and a short time later moved the terminus to Newcastle Emlyn. The railway continued to operate until 1973 when it was finally closed. Shortly afterwards a group of volunteers attempted to purchase part of the abandoned railway and preserve it as a standard gauge line; however, they were unsuccessful. In 1981, a group was able to purchase the

track bed and two years later, with the help of funding and labour from the Manpower Services Commission, a 2 ft narrow gauge line was laid and the Teifi Valley Railway was born. The line starts at Henllan and travels to what was the original terminus at Pontprenshitw, a place which literally means 'shaky wooden bridge' named after the original wooden structure there. Since then there have been two extensions, one to Llandyfriog and the other further on to the current end of the line referred to as 'Riverside'. There is a café and shop at Henllan where a new platform has recently been constructed.

What to see locally: It was in 1188 that Gerald the Welshman (w. *Giraldus Cambrensis*) travelled through Wales with the Archbishop of Canterbury, Baldwin, who was on a preaching mission in order to secure recruits for Richard the Lionheart's second crusade. The pair visited the area of the Cenarth Falls (GPS: 52°3′23.30″N 4°31′32.98″W) and Gerald describes the Church of St Llawddog, the mill with its bridge, the fish-lake, an orchard and a beautiful garden, all of which could be seen on a strip of land running along the banks of the River Teifi. It is suggested by him that the salmon leap was hewn out of the solid rock by the bare hands of the 6th century St Llawddog, who, born *circa* 525, was the patron of four churches in Wales. The Teifi, even in those times, was considered to be one of the best, if not the best river for salmon in the whole of Wales. It is recorded, for example, that over 100 salmon were taken in a single morning as they attempted to leap the falls on their way up river to spawn. (For more see www.visitcenarth.co.uk)

Neighbouring railways: The Gwili Railway, another heritage railway further down on the same original route (*see previous entry*).

Alan George being prepared alongside the new platform at Henllan for its first journey of the day on 1st August, 2009.   *Author*

36 Llanelli & Mynydd Mawr Railway (L&MMR)

Location: Cynheidre, six miles north-west of Llanelli.
GPS: Cynheidre: 51°44'39.59"N 4°11'17.66"W.
OS map reference: Cynheidre: SN495075.
Operator: Llanelli & Mynydd Mawr Railway Company Ltd.
Contact details: Llanelli & Mynydd Mawr Railway, c/o Des Thomas, 6 Capel Isaf Road, Llanelli, Carmarthenshire SA15 1QD. E-mail: des@thomasdes.wanadoo.co.uk
Route: A long term objective is to develop a railway line from Llanelli to Tumble, approximately 12 miles. In the meantime it is hoped to open the line in short stages with the first section being about one mile in length at Cynheidre.
Gauge: Standard.
Traction: Operational rolling stock includes a two-car class '117', a spare (non-operational) class '107' dmu vehicle and a 1965-built Sentinel diesel shunter No. 10222. The 1906-built 0-4-0 saddle tank steam locomotive No. 1498 *Desmond* is currently undergoing major overhaul at the Llangollen Railway.
Website: www.lmmrcoltd.sg5.co.uk
Operating dates: Not yet operating. Follow the progress on the main website and the related photo site at lmmrcoltd.fotopic.net
History of the Railway: The Carmarthenshire Tramroad was the first public operating railway established by statute in 1802 with the first trains running in 1803. Initially built as a tramway the traction was at that time provided by horses. The introduction of the line allowed for coal extracted locally to be transported to the Sandy area and to Llanelly Docks.* In 1798, the Stradey Iron Works was opened and by the spring of 1803 was receiving its coal, ironstone and limestone for the furnaces via the Carmarthenshire line. In 1844, the company had closed and so had the line which remained out of service for the following 30 years. At a meeting chaired by the local MP in 1880 it was decided to re-open the line and extend it to Cross Hands. The railway recommenced operations in 1883 run by a newly-formed company, the Llanelly & Mynydd Mawr Railway. This company operated for almost 40 years before being taken over by the GWR. Following the nationalization of the railways in 1948, the line became part of British Railways Western Region. The line continued as the principal conduit for the transport of coal from the Gwendraeth Valley until the closure of the Cynheidre Colliery in 1989. For more on this story read M.R.C. Price's book (*see Bibliography*).
History of the project: Today's LMMR was established as a non-profit making company in April 1999 with the aim of reinstating services on what is said to be Britain's first public railway operating under statute, the Carmarthenshire Tramroad. A heritage centre is planned which will tell the story of local industry which the railway served. The scheme is utilizing derelict land on the site of the former colliery at Cynheidre which has been owned by the LMMR since 2005. Work at the site at Cynheidre has already begun with the first project being the erection of a locomotive shed. The focus now is to achieve a running line of about one mile served by a platform and the locomotive shed. In addition to the heritage centre, it is intended there will be a gift shop and café. Following on the development of Cynheidre to Cynheidre North, the second stage will address two connections, i.e. Cynheidre to Sylen Bridge and Cynheidre to Swiss Valley. The third stage is to create the overall

* Llanelly is the original spelling, the 'y' now having been replaced with an 'i'.)

No. 1498 *Desmond* taken at the MOD site at Llangennech near Llanelli in 18th June, 2005. The locomotive is currently undergoing a programme of restoration at the Llangollen locomotive works prior to going into service in due course at Cynheidre.   *Des Thomas*

link from Llanelli to the edge of Tumble but this is very much a long term objective. *What to know locally*: Llanelli, which in English means Church of St Elli, is an attractive town at the mouth of the River Loughor, 13 miles west of the city of Swansea and 12 miles east of Carmarthen. For rugby fans it is the home of the famous Scarlets team. Llanelli grew significantly in the 18th and 19th centuries with the mining of coal and later tin. By the latter half of the 19th century the town had become a significant producer of tin earning the title 'Tinopolis'. The closure of the coal mines followed by the decline in steel production caused by competition from overseas meant that Llanelli, like many other towns in South Wales, saw a significant and sustained economic decline from the late 1970s onwards.

What to remember locally: In the early years of the 20th century there was a period of great social unrest in Britain. In Wales particularly there were strikes by coal miners in Tonypandy and by seamen in Cardiff. In 1911, a national railway strike brought chaos necessitating troops to be deployed to keep the trains operating. On one day in the August, strikers held up the trains at a level crossing in Llanelli. The next day a similar protest occurred and troops were summoned to clear the line. The Riot Act was read following which shots were fired and two young men, Leonard Worsell and John John, fell dead shot by soldiers from the Lancashire Regiment. Later that same day, a crowd attacked the home and business premises of one of the magistrates present at the level crossing incident. In a separate occurrence some railway trucks carrying detonators were set on fire causing a huge explosion in which four people were killed and many others were injured. For more on this tragic day in Llanelli's history read John Edwards' account (*see Bibliography*).

Neighbouring railways: The West Wales and the Heart of Wales lines.

Comments: This is an exciting project which will hopefully become not only a prosperous tourist attraction, but also an educational resource for future generations. This enterprise is well-worth supporting but is in desperate need of volunteers.

37 West Wales Line - Cardiff Central to Swansea

Locations: The cities of Cardiff and Swansea.
GPS: Cardiff: 51°28'52.71"N 3°10'49.79"W. Swansea: 51°37'13.61"N 3°56'47.90"W.
OS map references: Cardiff: ST186765. Swansea: SS657938.
Operator: Arriva Trains Wales and First Great Western.
Timetable: Arriva No. 3.
Route: Cardiff Central to Swansea via Pontyclun, Llanharan, Pencoed, Bridgend, Pyle, Port Talbot Parkway, Baglan, Briton Ferry, Neath, Skewen and Llansamlet, a distance of 42 miles.
Journey time: Just under one hour by First Great Western and by Arriva Trains.
Website: www.firstgreatwestern.co.uk and www.arrivatrainswales.co.uk
Operating dates: Year-round with frequent services delivered by both railway companies. It is unusual to have to wait longer than 20 minutes for a connection.
Railway constructions of interest: Cardiff Central railway station (w. *Caerdydd Canolog*) is the largest and busiest station in Wales and is one of the major stations in Britain's rail network, being the tenth busiest outside London. In the early 1840s the then South Wales Railway (SWR), which operated between 1844 and 1862, was searching for a suitable site to construct a railway station. However, the intended area, which is now the site of Cardiff Central railway station, was prone to flooding. Isambard Kingdom Brunel's response was not to find an alternative site but rather to divert the River Taff further to the west thus creating a larger, safer and drier location. The station was opened by the SWR in 1850 and was rebuilt in 1932 by the Great Western Railway. It is now a Grade II listed building. Swansea station was also built by the SWR and opened in 1850. It has been renovated and extended several times in its lifetime but nothing now remains there of the original Victorian wooden-built station with its two platforms and galvanised iron roof.
What to see locally: Whilst Cardiff has only enjoyed city status for about 100 years there has been a castle here for almost 2,000 years. The first was believed to have been built by the Romans about AD 55. Over the centuries since those Roman times it has been modified, improved and renovated. Lancelot Brown (1716-1783) better known as 'Capability Brown', for example, had a hand in developing the gardens in the mid-18th century. The most extravagant change, however, was instigated by the 3rd Marquess of Bute, reputed at the time, the 1860s, to be the richest man in the world. The Marquess, employing the eccentric architect William Burges (1827-1881) turned the castle into a gothic fantasy. Within the gothic fairytale towers are opulent interiors, rich with murals, stained glass, marble, gilding and elaborate wood carving. Each room has its own special theme, including Mediterranean gardens, and Italian and Arabian decorations. The clock tower with its attractive colourful figurines is wonderful to see but for the author the ceiling of the Arab Room is just something else! William Burges also designed the late 19th-century fairytale-style castle north of Cardiff, Castell Coch. It was built on medieval remains, again for the 3rd Marquess of Bute; the imposing structure is easily seen from the M4 motorway. Like Cardiff Castle, it is lavishly decorated and furnished in the Victorian gothic style. A more recent attraction is the *Doctor Who Up Close* exhibition. Much of the television series, and its two spin-off shows, *Torchwood* and the *Adventures of Sarah Jane*, were filmed in Cardiff using locations such as the Millennium Stadium,

Class 'A1' No. 60163 *Tornado* heads for Swansea from London Paddington on a St David's Day special seen here on 1st March, 2010 west of Pencoed approaching Bridgend.   *Author*

The Grade II-listed Cardiff station as re-built by the Great Western Railway in 1932 seen here on a gloomy and wet day in late February 2010.   *Author*

A First Great Western service heading for Bridgend on 1st March, 2010.   *Author*

Queen's Arcade Shopping Centre and the Wales Millennium Centre, all places worth visiting in their own right.

Whom to remember locally: Richard Walter Jenkins was born at Pontrhydyfen, five miles north-east of Port Talbot, on 10th November, 1925 and died in Switzerland in August 1984 of a cerebral haemorrhage. He was better known as the actor Richard Burton having taken for professional reasons the surname of his schoolmaster, tutor and friend, Philip Burton.

Neighbouring railways: Barry Rail Centre and Tourist Railway.

An Arriva class '175' has not long left Llanelli on 9th July, 2009. Here it is seen from the main A484 looking over the leisure lakes and bird sanctuary between Pwll and Burry Port. Beyond the train can be seen the estuary of the River Loughor with the Gower Peninsula on the opposing bank.   *Author*

The Loughor railway viaduct built by Brunel and Fletcher is seen here on 9th July, 2010 with a local Arriva service. The Gower is in the background.   *Author*

38 West Wales Line - Swansea to Whitland

Locations: Swansea and Whitland.
GPS: Swansea: 51°37'13.61"N 3°56'47.90"W. Whitland: 51°49'10.10"N 4°36'52.16"W.
OS map references: Swansea: SS657938. Whitland: SN196164.
Operator: Arriva Trains Wales.
Timetable: Arriva No. 3.
Route: Swansea to Whitland via Gowerton, Llanelli, Pembrey and Burry Port, Pen-bre & Porth Tywyn, Kidwelly, Ferryside and Carmarthen, a distance of 44 miles.
Journey time: 1 hour 18 minutes.
Website: www.arrivatrainswales.co.uk
Operating dates: Daily with hourly services.
Railway constructions of interest: A railway bridge, west of Swansea (GPS: 51°39'46.21"N 4°4'54.87"W) carries the West Wales line across the River Loughor. The original structure was built completely in timber about 1860 by Brunel and Fletcher. The timber was later replaced by wrought iron and even later by steel plate. It is now a Grade II listed structure but is scheduled for renewal in 2012/2013. From the modern road bridge running close to this section of railway there are stunning views over the water to the Gower Peninsula. Nearby, at Landore in Swansea, Brunel also built a viaduct in 1850. At 1,829 ft (563 m.) it was his longest timber-constructed viaduct.

What to know locally: Developing originally as a Viking trading post, about three-quarters of Swansea is bordered by the sea. The Loughor Estuary, Swansea Bay and the Bristol Channel all offer attractive seascapes especially on the nearby Gower Peninsula, the beautiful Three Cliffs Bay being an outstanding example. The port initially traded in wine, hides, wool and cloth. Later, as the Industrial Revolution took hold in the 18th and 19th centuries, coal increasingly became an important commodity to transport by sea. Numerous works were also established locally to process arsenic, zinc and tin. Copper, however, was the big business, so much so that the city was often referred to as 'Copperopolis'. Swansea suffered badly in World War II from German bombing. The 'Three Nights Blitz' of February 1941 is still remembered locally when much of the city was destroyed. Whitland sometimes is described by some as the site of the first law-making Welsh Parliament. An assembly of lawyers and churchmen were brought together there in 930 by the King of Deheubarth, *Hywel Dda* (e. Hywel [or Howell] the Good) in order to codify traditional Welsh law. Whitland is known as the home of the elusive 'Whitland Trout' which is noted particularly for its eggs and oily scales.

Whom to remember locally: Dylan Marlais Thomas, Wales' greatest poet, was born in October 1914 in Swansea, and died in 1953 in New York. During his lifetime he wrote many poems, including *Fern Hill*, *The hunchback in the park* and, of course, *Do not go gentle into that good night*. He will be perhaps best remembered for writing *Under Milk Wood*, and the collection of stories, *Portrait of the Artist as a Young Dog*. Nearby on the Gower, the 'Red Lady of Paviland' was discovered in 1823 by the Revd William Buckland in one of the Paviland

An Arriva train passes by the lovely village of Penally, near Tenby, on 10th July, 2009.   *Author*

The former station building at Pembroke Dock is now a pub, unsurprisingly named 'The Station Inn'! The platform still serves the arriving and departing trains.   *Author*

limestone caves. The remains, which were fairly complete, are the oldest of a human being ever to have been found in the United Kingdom. Being of the Upper Paleolithic era, the male skeleton, dyed in red ochre, dates back 26,350 years give or take 550 years! When Revd Buckley discovered the remains he misjudged both the age and the sex. Being one who believed in the Creation he could not accept that the skeleton could be older than the Biblical Great Flood (i.e. between 1450 BC and 450 BC). He thought that it was female largely because it was found with decorative items, including perforated seashell necklaces and ivory jewellery. These decorative items combined with the skeleton's red dye caused him to think mistakenly that the remains belonged to a Roman prostitute or witch. It is now generally accepted that the remains are of a man and that he was probably no older than 21 when he died; it is also thought that in spite of his young age he may have been a tribal chieftain.
Neighbouring railways: Gwili Railway and the Llanelli & Mynydd Mawr Railway.

39 West Wales Line - Whitland to Pembroke Dock

Locations: Whitland and Pembroke Dock.
GPS: Whitland: 51°49'10.10"N 4°36'52.16"W. Pembroke Dock: 51°40'48.05"N 4°54'30.41"W.
OS map references: Whitland: SN196164. Pembroke Dock: SM965031.
Operator: Arriva Trains Wales.
Timetable: Arriva No. 3.
Route: Whitland to Pembroke Dock via Narberth, Kilgetty, Saundersfoot, Tenby, Penally, Manorbier, Lamphey and Pembroke Town, a distance of 27 miles.
Journey time: About 1 hour.
Website: www.arrivatrainswales.co.uk
Operating dates: Daily every two hours
Railway constructions of interest: The attractive former station building at Pembroke Dock, now a public house.
What to see locally: Pembroke Castle, with its construction beginning around 1093 by Arnulf de Montgomery, is an imposing fortress set on the banks of the Cleddau River estuary opposite on the other bank to the town and port of Milford Haven. The keep, built in the late 12th century, is an outstanding example with its massive cylindrical tower capped with an unusual stone dome. Today, the castle remains largely intact in spite of numerous attacks upon it over the centuries. Once it was the stronghold of major barons who shaped much of Britain's history but it is probably best remembered as the birthplace of Henry Tudor, later King Henry VII, father to Henry VIII and grandfather of Elizabeth I. Pembroke Dock was established in the early years of the 19th century and was, for over a hundred years, one of the most important shipbuilding centres in the country. Apart from a short-lived affair at nearby Milford, the Royal Naval Dockyard at Pembroke Dock was the only such establishment ever to exist in Wales. RAF Pembroke Dock was established in 1930 and during World War II became the world's largest operational flying boat base regularly deploying 'Sunderland' and 'Catalina' flying boats to seek

Fishguard ferry port on 27th August, 2009 with *Stena Europe* preparing to leave on the afternoon sailing. The connecting Arriva train can be seen alongside the shed. *Geraldine Evans*

A metal sign advertising the Fishguard route on display in the museum STEAM at Swindon. *Author*

out enemy submarines. This war also brought devastation to the town including what turned out to be Britain's biggest conflagration since the Great Fire of London when the Pennar oil tanks burned continuously for 18 days. There used to be a local ferry from Pembroke Dock (Hobbs' Point) to Neyland but this was replaced by the Haven (Toll) Bridge opened in 1975. In 1988, the route to Ireland was re-opened with the company, Irish Ferries, now undertaking two sailings each day to Rosslare. Tenby is a popular holiday resort. Its history goes back to the 13th century when it had its own town castle with protective walls. However, in 1260 Prince Llywelyn ap Gruffudd (sometimes spelt Gruffydd and known to the English as 'the Last') vividly demonstrated to the Earls of Pembroke the inadequacy of the protection by sacking the town.

40 West Wales Line - Whitland to Fishguard

Locations: Whitland and Fishguard.
GPS: Whitland: 51°49'10.10"N 4°36'52.16"W. Fishguard: 51°59'35.43"N 4°58'30.11"W.
OS map references: Whitland: SN196164. Fishguard Harbour station: SM951390.
Operator: Arriva Trains Wales.
Timetable: Arriva No. 3.
Route: Whitland (from Cardiff Central) to Fishguard direct.
Journey time: 42 minutes from Whitland and a total of 2 hours 20 minutes from Cardiff.
Website: www.arrivatrainswales.co.uk

The afternoon train from Fishguard leaves Whitland heading towards Cardiff on 9th July, 2009.   *Author*

Operating dates: Daily but infrequent with only two services each way per day arriving at Fishguard at 1315 hours and departing at 1327 hours and then during the night arriving at 0126 hours and departing at 0150 hours. These services connect with the two ferry services each day operated by Stena Line between the ports of Fishguard and Rosslare, each crossing taking about 3½ hours.

Railway constructions of interest: The Spittal tunnel to Wolfscastle, 242 yards in length was built by the Great Western Railway and opened in 1908 on a route which had partly been conceived by Brunel 50 years before. The year following the opening the tunnel saw many trains pass through carrying passengers keen to see Cunard's recently launched RMS *Mauretania* which had docked at Fishguard harbour.

What to see locally: In 1797, the Royal Oak public house in Fishguard saw the signing of the surrender by French forces following what was in fact the last invasion on land of Britain. An army of 1,400 French soldiers had landed at Carregwastad Head and had made some progress inland but within two days it was all over. The story is told in the 'Fishguard Tapestry', which was created for the 200th anniversary and is now on display in the Town Hall. Situated 15 miles south-west of Fishguard is the Cathedral (w. *Eglwys Gadeiriol Tyddewi*) of St David's (GPS: 51°52'52.68"N 5°15'57.51"W) in the county of Pembrokeshire on what is the most westerly point of Wales. The monastic community at St David's was founded by Saint David (*circa* AD 500-589), the Abbot of Menevia, but the cathedral as we know it today was not built until 1181. Prior to that, in 1123, Pope Calixtus II declared St David's a place of pilgrimage saying that two pilgrimages to St David's was equal to one to Rome, and three pilgrimages equal to one to Jerusalem. The Pembrokeshire Coast National Park and the magnificent coastal path is a delight to walkers.

Neighbouring railways: The Gwili and the Teifi Valley railways.

41 West Wales Line - Whitland to Milford Haven

Locations: Whitland and Milford Haven.
GPS: Whitland: 51°49'10.10"N 4°36'52.16"W. Milford Haven: 51°42'41.59"N 5°1'44.89"W.
OS map references: Whitland: SN196164. Milford Haven: SM900064.
Operator: Arriva Trains Wales.
Timetable: Arriva No. 3.
Route: Whitland to Milford Haven via Clunderwen, Claberston Road, Haverfordwest and Johnston, a distance of 28 miles.
Journey time: 44 minutes.
Website: www.arrivatrainswales.co.uk
Operating dates: Daily with services every two hours.
What to see locally: Milford Haven was founded as a whaling centre in 1793. Today, the port is the fourth largest in the United Kingdom in terms of tonnage handled. It is also important in the United Kingdom's energy supplies with several oil refineries and one of the biggest LNG (liquified natural gas)

terminals in the world. The natural harbour of the Milford Haven Waterway was used for several hundred years prior to the establishment of the town. It was often used as a staging point on journeys by sea to Ireland and even earlier had afforded shelter to the Vikings. As well as being well known as a safe port it was used as a base for several military operations including Henry II's invasion of Ireland in 1171 and Oliver Cromwell's own invasion of Ireland in 1649. Forces which have disembarked at Milford Haven include, in 1405, Jean II de Rieux, a Breton Lord and Marshal of France who brought reinforcements to support Owain Glyn Dŵr's uprising. In 1485, Henry Tudor landed here with a small force made up French and Scots to march on England. Henry, about to become Henry VII, later the same year defeated Richard III, the last King of the House of York, at the Battle of Bosworth field. This event earned Henry the distinction of being the last English king to gain his throne on the battlefield and for Richard III the last English king to be killed in battle.

Arriva's No. 175114 leaves Whitland Junction for Milford Haven on 9th July, 2009. The route off to left, near the Network Rail workers, goes down to Pembroke.   *Author*

42 Bridgend to Maesteg

Locations: Bridgend and Maesteg.
GPS: Maesteg: 51°36′31.01″N 3°39′37.49″W. Bridgend: 51°30′26.15″N 3°34′51.75″W.
OS map references: Bridgend: SS905805. Maesteg: SS855915.
Operator: Arriva Train Wales.
Timetable: Arriva No. 3.
Route: Bridgend to Maesteg via Wildmill, Sarn, Tondu and Garth, a distance of nine miles.
Journey time: 21 minutes.
Website: www.arrivatrainswales.co.uk
Operating dates: Daily every hour.
History: The origins of the present-day community in the Llynfi Valley go back to the late 1820s. At that time the area's considerable coal and iron-ore resources were developed and exploited on an industrial scale. In 1828, a 15-mile horse-drawn railway was completed between a newly-established harbour at Porthcawl and Garnlwyd in the Llynfi Valley. This was known as the Dyffryn Llynfi & Porthcawl Railway and was extended to the Coegnant district near to the head of the valley by 1830. The railway opened-up the district and prompted the formation of an iron company which, in 1826, began construction of a works on Maesteg Uchaf Farm, near Maesteg's present-day town centre. By 1831, two blast furnaces were operating and the first rows of workers' housing had been erected near the ironworks. About the same time one of the first zinc smelters in Wales was established on Coegnant Farm which was close to the northern terminus of the railway. The Llynfi & Ogmore Valley Railway (L&OVR) was created in June 1866 operating on standard gauge track as opposed to Great Western Railway's broad gauge. The L&OVR threatened to build a competing line to that of the GWR which partly contributed to the latter being forced to change to standard gauge over its whole route from Didcot. The line from Bridgend originally operated beyond Maesteg through Caerau and the Cymmer tunnel and on to Abergwynfi. Connections were made with the collieries in Abergwynfi and Glyncorrwg and there were junctions at Tondu and Cymmer linking with the east-west routes across the valleys of the Llynfi and Afan. The Maesteg branch line was closed in 1970 and with the closure of the Cymmer tunnel the connection with the Afan Valley was also lost. A vigorous campaign in the late 1980s and early 1990s succeeded in the re-opening of the line to Maesteg in 1992.
What to see locally: The Bridgend Heritage Coast is well worth visiting. One of the newest attractions in the area is Tondu Park, where conserved structures of a former Victorian ironworks can be seen. Nearby are the castles of Newcastle, Ogmore, and Coity which were established on the western limits of the Norman incursion into South Wales.
What to remember locally: Bridgend played an important part during World War II. It was 'home' to a Prisoner of War camp at Island Farm. Also at Bridgend was ROF Bridgend, a large munitions factory known as the 'Admirality'. As an overspill of the Woolwich Arsenal, at its peak it had 40,000 workers, many of whom were women bussed in from the Rhondda and the

The Arriva service utilizing dmu No. 150241 from Maesteg to Cardiff Central is photographed here passing the playing fields at Coytrahen, just north of Tondu, on 26th February, 2010. *Author*

other valleys. At the time it was the factory employing the largest number of workers ever in the UK. The earliest settlement in the Llynfi Valley was at the Bwlwarcau Iron Age hillfort near to Llangynwyd village, which is about two miles to the south-west of Maesteg. This site suggests that there was human settlement in and around Maesteg more than 2,000 years ago.

Neighbouring railways: Garw Valley Railway in conjunction with the Vale of Glamorgan Railway.

43 Valley Lines - Cardiff Central/Queen Street to Pontypridd

Locations: Cardiff and Pontypridd.
GPS: Cardiff: 51°28'52.71"N 3°10'49.79"W. Pontypridd: 51°36'4.15"N 3°20'59.63"W.
OS map references: Cardiff: ST186765. Pontypridd: ST075895.
Operator: Arriva Trains Wales.
Timetable: Arriva No. 5.
Route: Cardiff Central to Pontypridd via Cardiff Queen Street, Cathays, Llandaf, Ninian Park, Waun Gron Park, Fairwater, Danescourt, Radyr, Taffs Well, Ystrad Trefforest and Trefforest, a distance of just over 12 miles.
Journey time: About 23 minutes.
Website: www.arrivatrainswales.co.uk
Operating dates: Every day with frequent services every 10/20 minutes
Railway constructions of interest: At a third of a mile long, Pontypridd had at one time the longest platform of any railway station in the country. It was known as Newbridge station from 1840 to 1891. Brunel designed an impressive skew stone arch viaduct at Pontypridd, which spanned 110 ft over the River Rhondda; the viaduct is still in use today, although it has been supplemented by a second, parallel viaduct. A similarly-designed viaduct can be found at Quakers' Yard.

The viaduct crossing the River Rhondda at Pontypridd as photographed on 15th February, 2010.
Author

Pontypridd's old bridge. *Author*

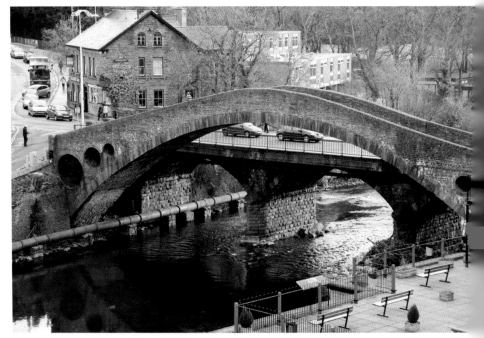

What to see locally: Pontypridd is renowned for its old bridge, which, when built, at 140 ft was the longest single-span bridge in Europe. It was completed in 1756 by the Reverend William Edwards (1719-1789) who took more than eight years and several attempts 'to get it right'. The Reverend Edwards was a Welsh Methodist Minister and a self-taught (!) architect and bridge engineer. The old bridge is perhaps his most famous creation but he also constructed bridges in Aberafan, Betws, Pontardawe and Usk. Whilst the old bridge survives, in the mid-19th century a second bridge was constructed alongside given that the original was just 'a bit too steep' to cross. 'Taffs Well' on this route derives its name from the adjacent river where there has been a natural hot spring (18.9 degrees celsius) used since Roman times.

Whom to have known locally: Sir Tom Jones OBE (born Thomas Jones Woodward in 1940) originates from Trefforest. To remind him perhaps of the 'green, green grass of home' Sir Tom has had an original red (not green!) UK telephone box erected in the grounds of his Los Angeles residence. Another musical connection for 'Ponty' (as it is affectionately known locally) is that it was here that the Welsh National Anthem *Hen Wlad Fy Nhadau* (The Land of My Fathers) was composed. In 1856 Evan James wrote the words and his son James composed the music.

Neighbouring railways: The Cardiff to Pontypridd line is the prime line serving the valleys. From Pontypridd station separate services run to Treherbert, Aberdare, and Merthyr Tydfil.

44 Valley Lines - Pontypridd to Treherbert

Locations: Pontypridd and Treherbert.
GPS: Pontypridd: 51°36'4.15"N 3°20'59.63"W. Treherbert: 51°40'30.07"N 3°32'13.45"W.
OS map references: Pontypridd: ST075895. Treherbert: SS945985.
Operator: Arriva Trains Wales.
Timetable: Arriva No. 5.
Route: Pontypridd to Treherbert via Trehafod, Porth, Dinas Rhondda, Tonypandy, Llwynpia, Ystrad Rhondda, Ton Pentre, Treorchy and Ynswen, a distance of just over 11 miles.
Journey time: 30 minutes.
Website: www.arrivatrainswales.co.uk
Operating dates: Daily with services every half hour.
History: The villages of Treherbert, Blaenrhondda and Blaencwm in the early 19th century consisted of no more than isolated rural farms and remote homes set in picturesque countryside. The latter two places were later located on the Rhondda & Swansea Bay Railway which ran north-westerly from Treherbert through the 443 yds-long Rhondda tunnel to Neath and Swansea. In 1845 the Cwmsaebren Farm (Treherbert) was purchased from William and Catherine Davies for a fee of £11,000, the plan being to extract the coal deposits which were believed to be present. Surveys began in 1850 and by 1853 the first seam of coal, in what later became known as the Bute Merthyr Colliery, was

The Treherbert-bound train passes under the A4233 road bridge at Porth on 13th July, 2009. *Author*

discovered at a depth of 125 yards. Production began in early 1855 and the first coal extracts were transported on an extended Taff Vale Railway from the Gelligaled station (Ystrad Rhondda) to the docks in Cardiff. With the opening of the pits and the supporting railway, there followed rapid increase in population and expansion of nearby villages.

Railway constructions of interest: Between 1885 and 1890, what was then the seventh longest tunnel in the United Kingdom was built by the Rhondda & Swansea Bay Railway under the Blaencwm mountain. The railway, which travelled through the Rhonnda tunnel, was closed in 1968, because of the condition of the tunnel, although alternative road transport was provided until 1970. The tunnel still exists underground but in the interests of safety the accesses have been sealed and are likely to remain so given the obvious dangers the tunnel continues to pose.

What to hear locally: Treorchy, two miles south of Treherbert, is the home of the world famous Treorchy Male Choir. There have been choirs in the Rhondda Valley for more than a 150 years but the Treorchy is probably one of the best known internationally. It was first formed in the Red Cow Hotel in the summer of 1883. It became a winner at a National Eisteddfod and later, in 1895, gave a Royal Command performance for Queen Victoria at Windsor Castle. Sadly, the effect of two World Wars and the Depression led the choir to being disbanded. However, it was re-formed in 1946 under the direction of John Haydn Davies who led the choir for the following 20 years and transformed it into the renowned international institution that it is today. The Treorchy Male Choir is a registered charity which devotes tens of thousands of pounds each year to worthwhile causes. More recently it has introduced a Junior Musician of the Year Competition which gives thousands of local children throughout the Rhondda the opportunity to perform.

Whom to remember locally: The Speaker of the House of Commons, George Thomas (1909-1997) was born in Port Talbot but was later brought up by his mother in the village of Trealaw just across the River Rhondda from the town of Tonypandy. When Speaker Thomas retired in 1983 he was created a hereditary peer taking the title 1st Viscount Tonypandy. As he died childless the peerage has since lapsed.

45 Valley Lines - Pontypridd to Aberdare

Locations: Pontypridd and Aberdare.
GPS: Pontypridd: 51°36′4.15″N 3°20′59.63″W. Aberdare: 51°42′49.22″N 3°26′42.32″W.
OS map references: Pontypridd: ST075895. Aberdare: SN998026.
Operator: Arriva Trains Wales.
Timetable: Arriva No. 5.
Route: Pontypridd to Aberdare via Abercynon, Penrhiwceiber, Mountain Ash, Fernhill and Cwmbach, a distance of a little over 12 miles.
Journey time: 31 minutes.
Website: www.arrivatrainswales.co.uk
Operating dates: Daily with services every half-hour.

Arriva's service with dmu No. 150255 approaches Mountain Ash station on 13th July, 2009 on its journey down to Barry Island.   *Author*

A view from the western slopes of Merthyr Vale overlooking Aberfan with a new school (*left of centre*) under construction in July 2009. The Arriva train can be seen at the foot of the opposing slopes. Looking at the lush greenery it is difficult to believe it was not that many years ago that this valley was heavily

Author

What to see locally: Dare Valley Country Park, set in its 500 acres, is a prime example of recovering land from the industrial past and, by converting it back to nature, providing a useful and attractive local amenity. Aberdare's disused coal-mining area has been so transformed into some of the most beautiful scenery in the valleys of South Wales.

What to know locally: On 25th January, 2008 the last coal mine in Wales, the Tower Colliery at Hirwaun, four miles beyond Aberdare, was closed. In 1864, the first drift named Tower had been opened on Hirwaun Common. Following the miners' strike of 1984/85 the pit came under threat and eventually British Coal closed it in April 1994 on the grounds that coal production there was no longer economic. The local miners were galvanized into action. £2 million was raised from their redundancy payouts and other sources and a buy-out group was formed which successfully bid for the ownership of the colliery. In January 1995, the colliery re-opened and continued successfully to mine coal for over a decade until it became clear that the coal seams were rapidly becoming exhausted.

Whom to have known locally: Born at nearby Trecynon in 1834 was the blacksmith Griffith Rhys Jones, commonly known throughout his musical life as 'Caradog.' He was the conductor of the famous *Côr Mawr*, the South Wales Choral Union, comprising some 460 voices; the choir twice won the first prize at London's Crystal Palace Choral Competitions in the 1870s. A statue to Caradog stands in the town's Victoria Square. Caradog is not an ancestor of Griff Rhys Jones, the comedian, writer, actor and television presenter, who was born in Cardiff in 1953. Another local personality is Dr Lyn Evans born in Aberdare in 1945. He is a Welsh scientist and project leader for the Large Hadron Collider (LHC) based in Cern, Switzerland. The LHC is the world's largest and highest-energy particle accelerator which it is intended will cause opposing particle beams of either protons or lead nuclei to collide. It is hoped that the results will address the most fundamental questions of physics and perhaps allow greater understanding of the deepest laws of nature.

46 Valley Lines - Pontypridd to Merthyr Tydfil

Locations: Pontypridd and Merthyr Tydfil.
GPS: Pontypridd: 51°36'4.15"N 3°20'59.63"W. Merthyr Tydfil: 51°44'51.01"N 3°22'41.03"W.
OS map references: Pontypridd: ST075895. Merthyr Tydfil: SO055065.
Operator: Arriva Trains.
Timetable: Arriva No. 5.
Route: Pontypridd to Merthyr Tydfil via Abercynon, Quakers Yard, Merthyr Vale (for Aberfan) Troed-y-rhiw and Pentre-bach, a distance of 12 miles.
Journey time: 29 minutes.
Website: www.arrivatrainswales.co.uk
Operating dates: Daily with services very half-hour.
History: The Merthyr High Street station was first opened on this site by the broad gauge Vale of Neath Railway in 1853 which 12 years later became part of

the Great Western Railway. It was used by trains of the Great Western, Taff Vale, London & North Western, the Brecon & Merthyr and the Rhymney railways. However, it is only the former Taff Vale line into the town which has survived, all the other routes having been closed between 1951 and 1962. The passenger facilities were rebuilt by British Rail on a corner of the original site in 1974 and improved again in 1996.

What to do locally: An enjoyable walk can be experienced by taking a path from the northern end of the Quakers Yard railway station platform crossing the line, over a field and down some steps to meet the Taff Trail (*see* www.tafftrail.org.uk) which is long-distance walk from Cardiff Bay to the Brecons. Here, one can take 'The Trevithick Trail', a foot/cycle path which follows the line of the former Trevithick Railway from Penydarren to Abercynon. From Quaker's Yard one can travel east on part of the Celtic Trail (National Cycle Route 47) to the spectacular Hengoed viaduct (*see next entry*).

What to remember locally: The Aberfan Disaster was a tragedy which shook the world. It took place in the early autumn of 1966 when, after several days of rain, at 0915 hours on Friday 21st October, 1966, the Pantglas tip of the Merthyr Vale Colliery slid down into the village killing 144 people, 116 of them children. The slide first destroyed a farm cottage in its path, killing all the occupants. At Pantglas Junior School, just below, the children had just returned to their classes after morning assembly. It was sunny on the mountain but foggy in the village with visibility down to about 50 yards. The slide engulfed the school and about 20 terraced houses in the village before coming to rest. Workers on the mountain had seen the start of the slide but were powerless to do anything about it as they could not raise an alarm because their telephone was not working - the cable connecting it had been repeatedly stolen! The Tribunal of Inquiry, under the chairmanship of Edmund Davies, later established, however, that the disaster happened so quickly that a telephone warning would not have saved lives. The Inquiry was forthright in apportioning blame for the disaster:

> ... the Aberfan Disaster is a terrifying tale of bungling ineptitude by many men charged with tasks for which they were totally unfitted, of failure to heed clear warnings, and of total lack of direction from above. Not villains but decent men, led astray by foolishness or by ignorance or by both in combination, are responsible for what happened at Aberfan. [It concluded] Blame for the disaster rests upon the National Coal Board. This is shared, though in varying degrees, among the NCB headquarters, the South Western Divisional Board, and certain individuals. ... The legal liability of the NCB to pay compensation of the personal injuries, fatal or otherwise, and damage to property, is incontestable and uncontested.

Whom to remember locally: The Merthyr Tydfil parliamentary constituency played a significant role in the struggle of the British working classes in the early part of the 20th century. In 1895, the founding father of the Labour Party, Keir Hardie, lost his first parliamentary seat for London's West Ham. For five years he was out of Parliament in a 'political wilderness' but continued campaigning vigorously to establish trades unions and gain Labour solidarity. In 1900, he won the Merthyr Tydfil parliamentary seat as the candidate for the then new Labour Representation Committee. For six years he was the only

The montage in a Merthyr Tydfil car park dedicated to the memory of Richard Trevithick.
Author

Labour member in Parliament but in the 1906 Parliamentary elections, a wind of change increased the numbers of the Labour representatives to 29. Keir Hardy kept the Merthyr seat until his death in 1915. Merthyr Tydfil is said to have been at one time the greatest iron-making town in the world. In 1804, the town witnessed the trial run on the tramway of the Penydarren Ironworks of the first steam locomotive in the world designed by Richard Trevithick (1771-1833). Whilst the trial was successful, regular services did not follow as the locomotive was found to be too heavy causing it to break the rails. Thereafter, the benefit of locomotive was not lost as it continued to operate but was restricted to static duties. A montage on the wall of the Tesco car park near to today's Merthyr Tydfil railway station marks the event. A monument in Merthyr also records the starting point of the tramway (for photograph *see page 16*).

Neighbouring railways: Brecon Mountain Railway and other Valley lines.

Comments: A visit to the cemetery and to the garden of remembrance in Aberfan is, as one might expect, a most moving event.

The final resting place for those children who tragically lost their lives in the Aberfan disaster in 1966.   *Author*

The Hengoed viaduct as photographed in February 2010. *Author*

Arriva's dmu No. 142077, and others, photographed from the Rhymney station platform on 12th July, 2009. *Author*

47 Valley Lines - Cardiff Queen Street to Rhymney and also branch line to Coryton

Locations: Cardiff, Queen Street and Rhymney.
GPS: Cardiff: 51°28′52.71″N 3°10′49.79″W. Rhymney: 51°45′34.30″N 3°17′7.11″W.
OS map references: Cardiff: ST186765. Rhymney: SO115075.
Operator: Arriva Trains Wales.
Timetable: Arriva No. 5.
Route: Cardiff Queen Street station to Rhymney via Heath High Level, Llanishen, Lisvane & Thornhill, Caerphilly, Aber, Llanbradach, Ystrad Mynach, Blackwood, Hengoed, Pengam, Gilfach Fargoed, Bargoed, Brithdir, Tir-phil and Pontllottyn a distance of just over 23 miles.
Journey time: 50 minutes.
Website: www.arrivatrainswales.co.uk
Operating dates: Daily all year round with services every 20 minutes.
Railway constructions of interest: Close to Ystrad Mynach is the Hengoed viaduct. This viaduct is a superb 16-arch construction stretching across the Rhymney Valley constructed for a railway that linked Pontypool to Swansea, via Aberdare and Neath. Built from 1853 onwards, the 845 ft-long viaduct was commissioned by the then Newport, Abergavenny & Hereford Railway and was designed by the engineer Charles Liddel. The railway which crossed the viaduct closed in 1964 but today it forms part of the Celtic Trail, part of the network of cycle routes across South Wales. The viaduct built on a small curve stands 120 ft above the valley.
What to remember locally: The worst ever coal-mining disaster in British history was in 1913 at Senghenydd, four miles north-west of Caerphilly, in which 439 men and boys lost their lives. This was not the only loss this community had suffered for 12 years earlier a disaster at the same mine had taken the lives of 81 men and boys.
What to see locally: Caerphilly Castle was built between 1268 and 1271 and is the largest castle in Wales, and second largest in Great Britain after Windsor Castle in Berkshire.
What to taste locally: Caerphilly is a white cheese which originated in the area around Caerphilly. However, it is now also made in England often on the English borders with Wales and in the south-west of England. It was not originally produced in Caerphilly but was sold at the town market there, hence capturing the name. Caerphilly is a crumbly cheese made from Hereford cows' milk, with a high fat content usually of 48 per cent. It has a mild taste accompanied by a not unpleasant slight sourness. It is said that the cheese was developed to help local coal miners who would eat the cheese as they would cake as a convenient way of replenishing the salt in their bodies lost through hard work underground. Real farmhouse Caerphilly production stopped during World War II as all milk had to go to the cheddar factories as part of the war effort. After the war these cheddar factories began making their own version of Caerphilly in order to help cash flow as the Caerphilly cheese matures much quicker than Cheddar. There are still a small number farms

making original Caerphilly which is dry in the middle and creamy around the edges. Annually the town of Caerphilly holds a three-day festival entitled 'The Big Cheese' (w. *Y Caws Mawr)* to celebrate the product.

Whom to remember locally: The comedian Tommy Cooper (1921-1984) was born in Caerphilly. Countless numbers will remember him for his own special brand of humour and for his tragic death on stage at Her Majesty's Theatre in a show that was broadcast live to millions on television. Perhaps surprisingly he had a morbid fear of the stage once remarking to his friend and fellow comedian Eric Sykes, 'People say I've only got to walk out on stage and they laugh. If only they knew what it takes to walk out on stage in the first place. One of these days I'll just walk out and do nothing. Then they'll know the difference'.

Neighbouring railways: An Arriva service also operates to Coryton via Heath Low Level, Ty Glas, Birchgrove, Rhiwbina and Whitchurch, a distance of four miles on a journey which takes 14 minutes.

The memorial to the comedian Tommy Cooper who was born in Caerphilly; part of Caerphilly Castle can be seen in the background.   *Author*

48 Valley Lines - Cardiff Central to Ebbw Vale Parkway

On 15th February, 2010 an Arriva dmu No. 150256 passes the Miners' Memorial recently established in Cwm further down the valley from Ebbw Vale.   *Author*

Locations: Cardiff, Central station and Ebbw Vale.
GPS: Cardiff: 51°28'52.71"N 3°10'49.79"W. Ebbw Vale: 51°46'53.99"N 3°12'20.20"W.
OS map references: Cardiff: ST186765. Ebbw Vale: SO169099.
Operator: Arriva Trains Wales.
Timetable: Arriva No. 3.
Route: Cardiff Central station to Ebbw Vale Parkway via Rogerstone, Risca & Pontmister, Crosskeys, Newbridge and Llanhilleth, a distance of over 37 miles.
Journey time: 57 minutes.
Website: www.arrivatrainswales.co.uk
Operating dates: Daily with services every hour.
History: Passenger services first operated on the line between Newport Courtybella and Blaina just before Christmas in 1850. An extension was opened to Newport Dock Street at the beginning of April 1852, with an extension from Aberbeeg to Ebbw Vale opening later the same month. Under the Beeching cuts the line was closed to passenger traffic at the end of April 1962. Happily, the line, after a tireless campaign, was restored for passenger services on 8th February, 2008.
Railway constructions of interest: The Crumlin viaduct, an outstanding feat of engineering on what was the Newport, Abergavenny & Hereford Railway, is now long gone but the Hengoed viaduct, although closed to rail traffic in 1964, has survived albeit now as a walk/cycleway (*see previous entry*).

What to see locally: In early 2010, the author observed that the former Ebbw Vale steelworks was in the process of being transformed into a vertical garden in time for the arrival of the National Eisteddfod. At Cwm the Miners' Memorial has two poems inscribed written by children from local schools which usefully illustrate how life environmentally has changed in recent years in Ebbw Vale. The first written by the children of Cwm school reads:

> *The Miners in cages*
> *Blackdust on their faces*
> *Work for their wages*
> *Working all day*
> *Morning till night*
> *Just to make sure their*
> *Kids are alright*
> *Mum makes a stew to last*
> *All week. Because they can't*
> *Afford to have many treats*
> *Now things are different*
> *The mine is no more*
> *Now people are better and*
> *Are no longer poor*

The second poem produced by the local Waunlwyd school is quoted in the Introduction.

Neighbouring railways: Pontypool & Blaenavon Railway, Brecon Mountain Railway and Pontypool Railway Museum.

49 Cardiff to Cardiff Bay

Locations: Cardiff and Cardiff Bay.
GPS: Cardiff: 51°28′52.71″N 3°10′49.79″W. Cardiff Bay: 51°27′51.73″N 3°9′41.98″W.
OS map references: Cardiff: ST186765. Cardiff Bay: ST193747.
Operator: Arriva Trains Wales.
Timetable: Arriva No. 5.
Route: Cardiff Queen Street station to Cardiff Bay station in Bute Street, a distance of about one mile.
Journey time: 4 minutes.
History: The original branch line was built and operated by the Taff Vale Railway until 1922 when it was amalgamated, together with the Rhymney Railway, into an enlarged Great Western Railway. With the development of the Cardiff Bay complex the line was given a new lease of life. In the summer of 2006 services to the Bay were sometimes provided by a 1950s British Rail class '121' diesel railcar known as a 'bubble car'. It continues to run, subject to remedial maintenance to ensure reliability, but only in the warmer months as there is no heating system installed to provide passenger and conductor/driver comfort!
Website: www.arrivatrainswalwes.co.uk and for the Bay www.cardiffbay.co.uk
Operating dates: Daily, every 12 minutes.

Railway constructions of interest: The former railway building complete with wooden canopy is now sadly in a rather dilapidated state. The existing platform is uninspiring which is rather surprising given that it is the only rail connection to the Welsh Assembly and other buildings on the Cardiff Bay complex.

What to see locally: Cardiff Docks was at one time the largest coal exporting port in the world. In the 1990s the dock complex was subject to a massive regeneration project. It has now become Europe's largest waterfront development. This was all made possible by the construction of a barrage which was completed in 1999. This allowed for the creation of a 500 acre freshwater lake with eight miles of waterfront which it was hoped would stimulate the future development of the Bay as a tourist and leisure destination. Already the Cardiff Bay complex is home to a number of attractions including Techniquest Science Discovery Centre, Craft in the Bay, Butetown History and Arts Centre, Goleulong 2000 Lightship, the Norwegian Church Arts Centre and the Wales Millennium Centre. The Welsh Assembly building (w. *Senedd*) is located at the Pierhead. If the traveller wants a change from the train a water-borne taxi service operates throughout the year from the Bay to the city centre and also to Penarth.

Whom to know locally: Shirley Veronica Bassey was born on 8th January, 1937, the youngest of seven children. Her mother, Eliza was married to Henry a Nigerian-born sailor and they lived in the dock area of Cardiff known as Tiger Bay.

The impressive Millennium Centre at the Cardiff Bay complex. *Author*

Jung's *Graf Schwerin-Lowitz* arrives at Pontsticill station on the afternoon of 12th July, 2009. Sheep on the line are the only serious hazards in this area!   *Author*

The splendidly well-maintained workshops at Pant with the 1930-built Baldwin in the background.   *Author*

50 Brecon Mountain Railway

Locations: Pant station, north of Merthyr Tydfil.
GPS: Pant: 51°47′11.32″N 3°21′48.93″W.
OS map reference: Pant station: SO059098.
Operator: Brecon Mountain Railway.
Contact details: Brecon Mountain Railway, Pant Station, Merthyr Tydfil, CF48 2UP. Telephone: 01685 722988. Fax: 01685 384854
Route: Pant station to a terminus (passengers may not alight) at the northern end of the Taf Fechan reservoir via Pontsticill halt.
Journey time: 1 hour 5 minutes including a 20 minute stop at Pontsticill.
Gauge: Narrow (1 ft 11¾ in.).
Steam Traction: There are six steam locomotives owned, two in operation. The 1908-built 0-6-2 *Graf Schwerin-Lowitz* by Arn Jung of Germany came to Brecon Mountain Railway in very poor condition from the former Mecklenburg-Pommersche Schmalspurbahn in the former East Germany. It is a well tank engine with auxiliary tender and weighs 14 tons. It underwent a complete rebuild and began operating on the line from 1981 onwards. In 1993 it benefited from a new boiler built in the workshops at Pant. To date it has travelled over 85,000 miles on the railway. *No. 2* was built by Baldwin of Philadelphia in 1930 but spent its professional life hauling limestone near Port Elizabeth in South Africa. Its career came to an unfortunate end in 1974 when it ran away driver-less for several miles before leaving the track. It was designated as a write-off by the insurers.

Jung's *Graf Schwerin-Lowitz* leaves Pant terminus on the afternoon of 12th July, 2009. The beautiful countryside of the Brecon Beacons is self-evident.   *Author*

Stormy clouds gather over the 1950-built Bagnall, *HM Dockyard Devonport No. 19* and its train on 12th July, 2009. *Caroline Jones*

The 1950-built Bagnall, *HM Dockyard Devonport No. 19* pushes its train up the incline towards the Whistle Inn on 12th July, 2009. *Author*

Later it was purchased as salvaged scrap and shipped to Liverpool. After a long rebuild in the railway workshops the 4-6-2 tender locomotive eventually came into service on the railway. *No. 26* is an 1898 Baldwin-built locomotive which ran for many years on the Mogyana Railway in Brazil. It is currently being rebuilt in the Pant workshops. Two new locomotives based on the original Baldwin drawings are also currently being constructed in the workshops which can be viewed from the walkway up to the platform at Pant station.

Website: www.breconmountainrailway.co.uk

Operating dates: A full programme is run from January to the end of October with five return journeys most days with an extra late afternoon service on public holidays. Additional services at weekends are operated in November and a comprehensive timetable is maintained on most days in December; Christmas Eve, Christmas Day and Boxing Day being the only exceptions. However, it is always wise to check first the state of current operations before travelling any great distance. The timetable on the railway's excellent website is particularly helpful.

What to know and see locally: Richard Trevithick (1771-1833) was the creator of the first steam locomotive in the world built in Merthyr Tydfil for the tramway of the Penydarren Ironworks (*for more see entry 46*). Near to the Brecon Mountain Railway is *Ogof Ffynnon Ddu* (e. The Cave of the Black Spring) which is one of the most extensive cave networks in Europe and at 1,010 ft is the deepest in Great Britain.

Neighbouring railways: Arriva services up to Merthyr Tydfil.

Comments: Visitors travel in all-weather observation coaches hauled by an immaculately well-maintained vintage steam locomotive through the outstanding natural beauty of the Brecon Beacons National Park. There are facilities for all the family including a children's play area and lakeside snack-bar at Pontsticill. There are licensed tea rooms and a souvenir gift shop at Pant as well as a picnic area overlooking the line. Up to four wheelchairs can be carried on each train but there is a need to book in advance by telephoning 01685 722988. This is a must-see area of Britain and definitely a must-do railway.

51 Pontypool & Blaenavon Railway

Location: Between Blaenavon and Brynmawr on the B4248 near Pontypool.

GPS: Pontypool: 51°42'1.61"N 3°2'19.66"W. Blaenavon: 51°46'20.27"N 3°5'8.57"W.

OS map references: Pontypool: SO286003. Pontypool & Blaenavon Railway: SO235095.

Operator: Pontypool & Blaenavon Railway.

Contact details: Pontypool & Blaenavon Railway Co., 'The Railway Shop', 13a Broad Street, Blaenavon, Torfaen, NP4 9ND. E-mail: info@PBRly.co.uk Telephone: 01495 792 263.

Route: Currently trains travel from Furnace Sidings to the Whistle Inn, a distance of three-quarters of a mile. About the time of the publication of this book there will have been a further extension completed southwards of one and a quarter miles to a new station in Blaenavon town.

Journey time: 17 minute round trip for the existing three-quarter mile journey. Overall timings for the two mile journey to be determined when the forthcoming extension is formally opened on an intended date in May.
Gauge: Standard.
Steam Traction: Locomotives: a 1950-built Bagnall *HM Dockyard Devonport* No. 19, 1917-built GWR '42XX' class, No. 4253 (awaiting restoration), 1926-built GWR '56XX' class, No. 5668 (awaiting restoration), 1945-built GWR '57XX' class, No. 9629 (under restoration), 1924-built Barclay 0-4-0ST *Harry* (awaiting boiler), 1935-built Barclay 0-4-0ST *Tom Parry* (future uncertain), 1944-built NCB Austerity class 0-6-0ST No. 8 (a slow restoration project), 1939-built Barclay Works 0-6-0ST No. 2074 *Llantarnam Abbey* (an ongoing restoration project) and 1900-built Avonside 0-6-0ST *Pontyberem* (presently non-operational).
Diesel Traction: English Electric type '3' (TOPS class '37/4') No. 37421, Brush A1A-A1A D5627 (class '31/1' No. 31203) *Steve Organ GM*, class '73/1' electro-diesel No. 73128 *OVS Bulleid CBE*, English Electric type '3' (class '37/2') No.37216, BR type '1', 0-6-0DM, No. D2141 ('03' class, No. 03141) plus a varied collection of industrial diesel locomotives.
Website: www.pontypool-and-blaenavon.co.uk (recently revised- 24.02.2010).
Operating dates: Weekends from Easter to early October
History: The line from Brynmawr to Blaenavon was originally built in 1866 by a railway company of the same name and leased to the London & North Western Railway for the purposes of transporting coal to the Midlands. Eight years later it was extended to meet the GWR at Abersychan and Talywain. Here the line continued down the valley through Pontypool to the coast at Newport. In 1923, the LNWR became part of the London, Midland & Scottish Railway. The line was closed to passengers in 1941 and for freight in 1954. However, the section of line from Blaenavon to Pontypool continued to be used for moving coal from Big Pit and other local mines until 1980. The track was then lifted from Cwmbran through Pontypool to just south of Blaenavon (High Level) station. On this closure, volunteers created the Pontypool & Blaenavon Railway Company (1983) Ltd and its support group the Pontypool & Blaenavon Railway Society. Trains began running in 1983 and have continued since. Exciting times are ahead for this developing railway.
Railway constructions of interest: Channel 4's *Time Team* visited Blaenavon in 2001 to search for the world's first railway viaduct. It was said to have had 10 arches and be 130 ft long and 32 ft 6 in. high. It had been built in 1790 to carry coal to, what was then, the new Blaenavon blast furnaces. Within 25 years of it being built, it had disappeared from the landscape with no record of it having been demolished. The *Time Team* did find the roof of the viaduct almost 49 ft down but it was found to be too dangerous to excavate further.
What to see locally: At Big Pit is the National Coal Museum which since 2000 has been a UNESCO World Heritage site. It is possible to experience a guided tour underground. (See www.world-heritage-blaenavon.co.uk or telephone: 01495 790311). Whilst in the area the preserved ironworks at Blaenavon are well worth visiting to learn more about the local iron industry. The Blaenavon Ironworks, incidentally, was used as the backdrop for the BBC's *Coal House* series in which the railway also featured. Built in 1788 it is one of the best-preserved ironworks in existence and is now a UNESCO World Heritage site.

The Blaenavon Ironworks Museum.   *Author*

Neighbouring railway interest: The Pontypool Railway Museum at Griffithstown.
Comments: There is ample free parking for cars and coaches at Furnace Sidings. Most trains can provide drinks and light refreshments. The Whistle Inn at the northern end of the line also provides restaurant facilities, a beer garden and children's playground on Sundays and on Bank Holidays in the season. The line is the highest and steepest in the country, climbing through a wild moorland landscape under the Coity mountain. Sheep are common. Mountain horses, the peregrine falcon and hen harrier, and even rare red kite can also been seen from the site. For the lepidopterist, the very rare small pearl-bordered fritillary is known to make occasional visits. Garn Lakes are within five minutes walk and which are the perfect spot for a gentle walk or a picnic after a ride on the train. Gifts, models and souvenirs are available at the shop, by the car park. If you are in the town call in at the gift and model shop at 13a Broad Street where a wider range of goods is available.

52 Pontypool Railway Museum

Location: Griffithstown, six miles north of Pontypool in Torfaen.
GPS: Griffithstown: 51°41′3.53″N 3°1′40.12″W.
OS map reference: Griffithstown: ST295995.
Operator: Owned and operated by Martin Fay.
Contact details: Griffithstown Railway Museum, Station Road, Griffithstown, Pontypool, Torfaen, NP4 5JH. Telephone: 01495 762908.
Operating dates: Seven days per week from 1000 to 1700 hours.
Tariff: £1.

The former GWR goods shed and car park to the museum at Griffithstown. *Author*

Some of the many nameplates and plaques displayed on the walls of the Griffithstown Museum. *Cogan Hall*, incidentally, was, until recently, stored in the open at Llynclys station of the Cambrian Heritage Railways awaiting restoration. However, the Board of the 6880 - Betton Grange (Society) Ltd at Llangollen (*see entry 15*) has purchased the locomotive with a host of spares. It is intended, however, that *Cogan Hall* will eventually be restored so they may want the nameplate back! *Author*

History: Griffithstown Railway Museum, opened in 2002, is a small museum housed in the old engine repair shed on Station Road, adjacent to the former Griffithstown railway station. This former Great Western Railway goods shed has been lovingly restored and now houses a fine collection of railway memorabilia and a model railway. In the museum you will find a cornucopia of railway treasures from local stations, including a complete station master's office. Incidentally, Griffithstown, boasting a proud railway heritage, was named after Henry Griffiths the first GWR station master at the nearby Pontypool Road station. In 1880, the town gained another railway association, when it became the birthplace of the trade union ASLEF (Associated Society of Locomotive Engineers and Firemen).

What to remember locally: The West Monmouth School was originally Jones' West Monmouth School and owes its existence to the charitable donations of William Jones who died in 1615 bequeathing his money to the Worshipful Company of Haberdashers for the foundation of a grammar school in Monmouth. The school was formally opened much later in 1898. Notable students include the actor Sir Anthony Hopkins and Alun Jones, later Lord Chalfont, a Foreign Office Minister under a Labour Government between 1964 and 1970. Edwin Stevens also attended the school. He is probably best remembered for inventing the hearing aid which was small enough so that it could be fitted in the outer ear. Winston Churchill was one of his distinguished clients.

What to see locally: The Pontypool Museum, located in a Georgian-era stable block, houses interesting artefacts including examples of the famous Pontypool Clocks designed and built by local horologist Charles Vaughan in the mid-18th century. Examples of the renowned Pontypool & Usk 'Japanware' are also displayed. Incidentally, 'japan' refers to the process of japanning rather than the country. This process is credited to Thomas Allgood of Pontypool who, in the late 17th century, searched for a corrosion-resistant coating for iron. He developed a recipe which included asphaltum, linseed oil and burnt umber! Once this rather bizarre concoction was applied to metal and heated, the coating turned black and proved to be extremely tough and durable.

Neighbouring railways: Pontypool & Blaenavon Railway. The Cardiff to Abergavenny and Shrewbury main line passes nearby.

53   Garw Valley Railway incorporating members of the former **Vale of Glamorgan Railway**

Locations: Pontycymer and Tondu, north of Bridgend.
GPS: Pontycymer: 51°36'42.09"N 3°35'3.45"W. Tondu: 51°32'47.08"N 3°35'51.07"W.
OS map references: Pontycymer: SS905915. Tondu: SS895845.
Operator: Bridgend Valleys Railway Company Ltd.
Contact details: Bridgend Valleys Railway Company Limited, T/A Garw Valley Railway, Pontycymer Locomotive Works, Old Station Yard, Pontycymer, Bridgend, CF32 8AZ. E-mail for business and project management: breesconsultants@aol.com and for membership matters: juliae.gilbert@yahoo.com
Route: Pontycymer to Tondu (proposed) a distance of five miles.

Arriva dmu No. 143604 arrives at Barry Island station on 16th February, 2010. The track to the right over the white fence with the gate is that which takes traffic down to the Barry Island engine sheds. *Author*

The engine sheds at Barry Island on 16th February, 2010. *Author*

Gauge: Standard
The project: The stated aim of the Garw Valley Railway (GVR) is 'to recreate for present and future generations a typical South Wales Valleys branch line by providing a working museum atmosphere based principally upon the traditions of the Great Western Railway just prior to nationalisation'. It is hoped to restore passenger train services between Pontycymer and Tondu within the next 10 years and possibly into Brynmenyn Industrial Estate where a National Railway Centre could be developed. In February 2009, the Vale of Glamorgan Railway (VGR) announced that it had negotiated a new home for itself with the Garw Valley Railway. Whilst the VGR still exists as an entity, members of both the GVR and the former VGR are now one and the same being based at the Pontycymer site. Currently all members are working together to establish a working railway along the five mile stretch of line which was closed to passengers in 1953 and to freight in 1997. It is understood that the former VGR still owns an 0-6-0ST *Pamela* currently outhoused in Lincolnshire. It is hoped that she will return to the GVR in the near future. When she does in effect she will be coming home in that she was originally based at NCB Maesteg, a few miles away in the next valley. The 1952-built Robert Stephenson & Hawthorn 0-4-0ST No. 7705 has been purchased by a consortium and has now moved to Pontycymer to finalize its restoration. It is planned to use a class '108' dmu to run operations along the initial stretch of line between Pontycymer and Llangeinor, a distance of about three miles; it is hoped these passenger services will start sometime in 2010. The route is also known as *The Daffodil Line*.
Website: www.garw-railway.co.uk
Operating dates: To be announced.
Neighbouring railways: West Wales line from Cardiff to Swansea.

54 Barry Rail Centre and Tourist Railway

Location: Barry, Vale of Glamorgan
GPS: Barry Island: 51°23′32.85″N 3°16′20.75″W.
OS map reference: Barry Island: ST115669.
Operator: Cambrian Transport Ltd.
Contact details: The Station Buildings, Barry Island, Vale of Glamorgan CF62 5TH. Telephone: 01446 748816.
Website: www.cambrianco.co.uk
Route: Barry goods depot, now Waterfront station, to Barry Island station, a distance of just under one mile.
Journey time: Varies depending on vehicle used. However, as a guide Arriva's dmu services take six minutes to reach Barry Island station from Barry station.
Gauge: Standard.
Operating dates: Trains are operated at weekends from April to early September with extra at Easter, Bank Holidays, Guy Fawkes Night and Christmas.
Traction: Diesel and steam locomotives and other vehicles (to be announced).
History: The tourist railway at Barry was created by the Vale of Glamorgan Council and the Welsh Development Agency in 1996, and continually

developed and expanded over the years since then. Originally operated by the Vale of Glamorgan Railway Company, the railway is now under the control of Cambrian Transport Ltd who said,

> We are delighted that Cambrian Transport has been selected as the preferred bidder by the council. Our inclusive and exciting bid will lead to major investment in the rail infrastructure at Barry, and make a significant contribution to the ongoing regeneration of the town. We have a strong desire to work with groups and volunteers in Barry to secure a sustainable future for heritage activities, and we will seek to ensure that there are as many opportunities for local people to be involved as possible.

The Railway: The site has been renamed the 'Barry Rail Centre', and the 'Tourist Railway' is part of the overall use of the site. Other uses will include a skills training operation, a commercial rail engineering operation, and a heritage restoration facility. Cambrian intends to develop each of these uses over the course of its lease. The 'Tourist Railway' can be accessed via the main line Barry Island station, or, if arriving by car, parking is available at the railway's own Barry Waterfront station. A new station café is being planned for the Barry Island station buildings, and tickets for services can be purchased from the café, or on board the train if joining at the Waterfront station. Heading north from Barry Island the line crosses the causeway bridge parallel to Network Rail line before taking a sharp right-hand turn and splitting into two branches, one leading up to Hood Road (the Waterfront), the other heading past Woodham Halt to the new terminus at Gladstone Bridge next to the supermarkets.

What to remember locally: The railway runs close to the site of the former Woodham Brothers scrapyard, famous in UK heritage railway circles. As a matter of interest parts of the line, particularly around the Plymouth Road and Barry Island areas, were used as locations for some scenes in the *Doctor Who* episodes of *The Empty Child* and *The Doctor Dances* in January 2005. The railway has also been use for filming locations for other television dramas.

'The Barry 10': This euphemism has been given to the collection of 10 locomotives remaining when Dai Woodhams retired from his scrapyard in 1989. The collection was purchased for the Wales Railway Centre Project with the support of the then Glamorgan County Council and financial assistance from the National Heritage Memorial Fund. The engines plus two tenders were initially moved to Cardiff, but when the Wales Railway Centre Project failed the collection was returned to Barry and joined by an eleventh engine, GWR 2-6-2T No. 5538, which was on static display on the promenade on Barry Island and certainly not benefiting from effects of salt and sea air. The engines were stored first in protective storage and later moved to the former locomotive shed at Barry. Since 1998 various studies have been undertaken followed by protracted discussions to decide what best to do with this important and sizeable collection of railway history. A strategy was devised by Cambrian Transport and adopted in outline in 2003. There followed much work to secure the formalized approval of the Vale of Glamorgan Council and other stakeholders as well as seek out partners to take forward restoration projects. Early success was achieved following the agreed removal of GWR 4-6-0 No. 7927 *Willington Hall* and LMS 2-8-0 No. 48518 to the Llangollen Railway to facilitate the 1016 *Vale of Glamorgan* and 6880 *Betton Grange* projects. Following on

this success another agreement was struck with Hugh Shipton and Mike Little to restore GWR 2-6-2Ts Nos. 5538 and 5539. Incidentally, by the terms of these various agreements it is likely that all four locomotives in time will be seen operating on the Barry Tourist Railway. By 2009, Vale of Glamorgan Council, encouraged by the achievements so far made, accepted the bid by Cambrian Transport to become the new operator of the Barry Tourist Railway. Over time, prior to this, many expressions of interest had been stated in acquiring some of the other remaining locomotives for full restoration or static display projects. Some of this interest is being, or will be, pursued. One attractive and innovative bid which is now being explored, having been agreed in principle by the Vale of Glamorgan Council, is for the Mid-Hants Railway 'Watercress Line' to exchange its turntable for BR 2-6-4T No. 80150. If this proposal comes to fruition it would permit the Barry Rail Centre to develop a main line depot capable of receiving and servicing main line passenger excursion trains; a fully operational turntable is viewed as a 'must' for this objective. The future for all the 'Barry 10' locomotives is now secure. The following traction will eventually emerge after restoration (much of which will be undertaken at the Barry Rail Centre): Great Western Hawksworth 4-6-0 No. 1016 *County of Glamorgan*, Churchward '2221' 'County' class 4-4-2T, Churchward '38XX' 'County' class 4-4-0, '47XX' class 2-8-0 express tender engine, GWR 2-6-2 tanks Nos. 5538, 5539 and 6686, No. 6880 *Betton Grange*, LMS 'Black Five' class 4-6-0 No. 44901, LMS 2-8-0 '8F' class No. 48518, BR 2-6-4T No. 80150 and, finally, BR 2-10-0 tender locomotive No. 92245 which will be retained for display as an example of a 'Barry Hulk'. There is an exciting future ahead for Barry and its railway centre and one well worth following over the coming years.

Neighbouring railways: The West Wales Line (Cardiff to Swansea) and Arriva's Vale of Glamorgan line (Cardiff to Bridgend via Rhoose for Cardiff Airport and to Penarth).

55 Vale of Glamorgan Line - Cardiff Central to the South and West

Locations: Cardiff and Bridgend.
GPS: Cardiff: 51°28'52.71"N 3°10'49.79"W. Bridgend: 51°30'26.15"N 3°34'51.75"W.
OS map references: Cardiff: ST186765. Bridgend: SS905805.
Operator: Arriva Trains Wales.
Timetable: Arriva No. 5.
Routes: Cardiff Central/Queen Street to Grangetown and Cogan Junction and then 1) to Dingle Road and Penarth (4 miles) where it terminates; or, 2) to Barry Docks and Barry for Barry Island; and, 3) continuing on via Rhoose-Cardiff International Airport and Llanwit Major to Bridgend (32 miles), where it rejoins the West Wales main line. The Vale of Glamorgan Line proper starts at Barry.
Journey time: From Cardiff Central the journey takes 15 minutes to Penarth, 24 minutes to Barry station plus 6 minutes to Barry Island, 30 minutes to Rhoose Cardiff International Airport, 40 minutes to Llanwit Major and 59 minutes to Bridgend.
Website: www.arrivatrainswales.co.uk
Operating dates: Daily with frequent services.

Porthkerry viaduct with its 13 arches and standing at 110 ft high was opened on 1st December, 1897. This picture of the viaduct complete with an Arriva two-car dmu was taken on 16th February, 2010. *Author*

History: The Vale of Glamorgan line was originally opened in 1885 and at that time was part of the Barry Railway Company; it was absorbed into the Great Western Railway in 1923. From Cogan Junction the branch line used to continue beyond Penarth following the coast line through Lavernock and Sully before rejoining the main part of the line again at Cadoxton. However, this section fell foul of the Beeching cuts in the early 1960s. The Barry to Bridgend section suffered a similar fate, closing to passengers in 1964. However, more recently, this route has been restored following the tireless efforts of local residents and the pressure group 'Railfuture'. A vigorous campaign for a re-opening of the line led eventually to the award of a £17m project and in 2005 the route was re-opened to passenger traffic.

Railway constructions of interest: The Porthkerry viaduct (GPS: 51°23'48.07"N 3°19'3.07"W. OS: ST095675), near to Barry, standing at 110 ft high with 13 arches was opened on 1st December, 1897. However, disaster struck on 10th January the following year when subsidence, poor cement and faulty workmanship caused one of the piers to slip. Part of the line had to be closed. A temporary loop line was built 2½ miles to the north whilst the repairs were carried out.

What to see locally: It is possible, in a day, to take a walk around Wales from Celtic times to the present day! Incredible as that may seem it can be achieved by making a visit to St Fagans which is one of Europe's leading open-air museums and Wales's most popular heritage attraction. The facility has been open to the public since November 1948. The museum stands in the grounds of the magnificent St Fagans Castle and gardens, a late 16th century manor house which was donated to the people of Wales by the Earl of Plymouth in 1946. During the past 60 years, over 40 original buildings from different historical periods have been re-erected in the 100-acre parkland. Among them there are houses, a farm, a school, a chapel and a splendid Workmen's Institute. It is well worth a visit allowing a full day to take it all in. There is an entry charge. St Fagans is located four miles to the west of Cardiff city centre, just off the main A4232.

What to remember locally: Barry Island for a long time was an important port used for the transport of coal. However, it has another claim to fame in that was here that Billy Butlin was inspired to develop his holiday camps. In Barry, as a young man whilst on holiday he endured the unhappy experience, regardless of the weather, of being locked out of his bed and breakfast lodgings all day by his landlady, a not uncommon experience here and elsewhere. Consequently, in 1935 he built his first holiday camp at Skegness, where people could stay in all day if they wished. His ninth and last holiday camp was built at Barry in 1966 but closed 20 years later.

Neighbouring railways: Barry Rail Centre and Tourist Railway and the West Wales line from Cardiff to Swansea.

56 Cardiff Central to Abergavenny for Hereford

Locations: Cardiff, Abergavenny and Hereford.
GPS: Cardiff: 51°28′52.71″N 3°10′49.79″W. Abergavenny: 51°49′29.42″N 3°1′15.29″W. Hereford: 52°3′21.57″N 2°43′3.17″W.
OS map references: Cardiff: ST186765. Abergavenny: SO302143. Hereford: SO515405.
Operator: Arriva Trains Wales.
Timetable: Arriva No. 2.
Route: Cardiff Central to Abergavenny via Newport, Cwmbran, and Pontypool & New Inn. Between Pandy and Pontrilas the line straddles the boundary between Wales and England although there are no stops on this section. Trains continue to Shrewsbury in England via Hereford, Leominster, Ludlow and Craven Arms. This route on the English side is through what is known as the Welsh Marches, the borderlands between Wales and England. It is a most scenic route especially through the western parts of Shropshire and Herefordshire with Caer Caradoc, the Long Mynd and the Stiperstones to experience and enjoy.
Journey time: 41 minutes.
Website: www.arrivatrainswales.co.uk
Operating dates: Daily with services hourly with more at peak times.
Local Art History: A superb picture depicting a viaduct entitled *Abergavenny Bridge Monmouthshire Clearing Up After A Showery Day* was painted between 1797-98 by J.M.W. Turner. Sadly, the viaduct has now long gone but the picture is worth seeing if one can, probably most easily with the aid of Google™.
What to see locally: Offa's Dyke is an earthwork which was built by Offa, who was King of Mercia between 757 and 796. The dyke forming a boundary between England and Wales was constructed in an attempt to quell the marauding Welsh. It is the longest monument in Britain running for 182 miles from Prestatyn in the north to Sedbury, near Chepstow in the south. It is said that Offa required all men on the Mercian (English) side to contribute to the construction of the earthwork but they were given a choice. They could either send food to the construction workers or they could build a length of four feet of the dyke themselves! Much of the dyke is still traceable but not all of it can now be seen owing to the impact of farming for well over a millennium.

On leaving Newport, trains heading for Abergavenny and beyond negotiate St Julian's girder bridge crossing the River Usk near to the former Roman settlement at Caerleon. The photograph was taken early in the morning of 27th February, 2010. *Author*

Arriva's class '175' dmu No. 175008 photographed near Llanover heading for Abergavenny on 13th July, 2009. *Author*

57 West Wales Line - Cardiff Central to Chepstow and **to Bristol via Severn Tunnel**

Locations: Cardiff and Chepstow.
GPS: Cardiff: 51°28′52.71″N 3°10′49.79″W. Chepstow: 51°38′22.07″N 2°40′41.00″W.
OS map references: Cardiff: ST186765. Chepstow: ST533940.
Operator: Arriva Trains Wales and Cross Country Trains.
Timetable: Arriva No. 3.
Route: Cardiff Central to Chepstow via Newport, Severn Tunnel Junction and Caldicot. Trains continue beyond Chepstow to Lydney (convenient change for the Dean Forest Railway running from Lydney Junction, *see entry 59*) Gloucester and Cheltenham Spa. The other route here is also from Cardiff Central but at the Severn Tunnel Junction trains bound for Bristol disappear into the Severn Tunnel. The tunnel which is 4.35 miles long was built between 1873 and 1886. A staggering total of 76,400,100 bricks and 36,794 tons of Portland cement were used in the tunnel's construction. For more about the history of the tunnel and its construction read John Daniel's comprehensive and fascinating account recorded at www.greatwestern.org.uk/severn1.htm In early December 1991 the tunnel was the scene of a serious accident when the 0830 hours High Speed Train (HST) from London Paddington to Cardiff Central was stopped at a signal at the entrance to the Severn Tunnel. On telephoning the signalman, the driver was told of a signal failure but was given permission to proceed into the tunnel but with caution. Three miles into the tunnel, the train was struck from behind by a class '155' 'Super-Sprinter' travelling *en route* from Portsmouth to Cardiff. A total of 185 passengers were injured, including five seriously, but fortunately no one was killed. The tunnel is not the only railway crossing of the Severn Estuary. In 1875, construction began on the Severn railway bridge which was completed in 1879. The bridge continued to take rail traffic until disaster struck in the late evening of 25th October, 1960. For more on this disaster *see entry 59*.
Journey time: 48 minutes by Arriva and 36 minutes by Cross Country Trains.
Websites: www.arrivatrainswales.co.uk and www.crosscountrytrains.co.uk
Operating dates: Daily with frequent services every half hour.
Railway constructions which were of interest: Brunel's 1852-built great tubular bridge over the River Wye at Chepstow was a precursor to his masterpiece, the Royal Albert Bridge over the River Tamar which was completed in 1859, the year of his death. His foresight in allowing for slight movement of the suspension chains against the supports to ease the stresses, ultimately, however, led to this bridge's downfall. Over a hundred years later, a weakening of the structure necessitated its part replacement in 1962.
What to see locally: The Newport transporter bridge (*see next entry*). Just over four miles from Chepstow is Tintern Abbey (OS: SO535005). It was a Cistercian abbey founded in 1131 in the beautiful Wye valley and is a remarkably complete abbey church. It was rebuilt in the late 13th and early 14th centuries, with extensive remains of the cloisters and other monastic buildings still to be seen. Whilst at Tintern a visit to the restored railway station is a must. The railway, which was originally served by the station, was closed to passenger traffic in

An EWS class '66' locomotive No. 66020 locomotive leads an empty freight service over the River Usk on 27th February, 2010. The photograph gives the impression that the Newport railway bridge is a brightly-painted construction. Far from it, the bridge in the foreground is in fact the Clarence Place road crossing. The railway bridge behind is much less exciting! Part of the ruined Newport Castle can be seen on the left.   *Author*

Whilst it is not the prettiest structure to admire, this tubular bridge over the River Wye built by Brunel has an important history (*see text*).   *Author*

The beautiful 1816-built road bridge over the River Wye which spans the second highest tidal range in the world. It can exceed 46 ft in a single day. The highest, as a matter of interest, is caused by the tides on the Petitcodiac River in New Brunswick, USA. The photograph was taken on a stormy day in late February 2010. *Author*

West of Newport a First Great Western service overtakes a service composed of three passenger carriages topped and tailed by two class '67s' on 15th February, 2010. *Author*

A view of the transporter bridge as photographed on 16th February, 2010.   *Author*

Newport Transporter Bridge's 'gondola' suspended over the River Usk.   *Author*

1959 and the route completely abandoned in 1964. In recent times the site has been lovingly restored with the attractive station building now playing host to a small café, apparently serving delicious apricot flapjacks! The handsome signal box has also been restored and now is a small crafts shop. The original trackbed has been grassed over where visitors can enjoy a picnic and nearby is an area where children can play. The trackbed also offers a delightful wooded walk leading up to Llandogo. The ever attractive River Wye is nearby. The station site is open seven days a week between 1030 and 1730 hours. Chepstow Castle, sited on top of cliffs overlooking the River Wye (the boundary between Wales and England) is the oldest surviving stone fortification in Britain. It was built from 1067 at the behest of the Norman Lord William FitzOsbern who was a relative and close adviser to William the Conqueror. For his loyalty FitzOsbern was created Earl of Hereford. Chepstow was the southernmost of a chain of castles built along the English-Welsh border. Each year Chepstow racecourse hosts the Welsh Grand National, a testing handicap chase of three miles and about five and a half furlongs. It usually takes place in December between Christmas and New Year. The Welsh Grand National, however, was first run in 1895 at the Ely racecourse in Cardiff, where it remained until the closure of that course in 1939. The race moved to its present venue in Piercefield Park at Chepstow in 1949.

Comments: There is an active campaign at Chepstow to have more train services and/or more of the passing-through trains to stop there. This would benefit not only the local sizeable population but also the many hikers/cyclists wishing to visit the glorious Wye Valley entering by way of the southern approach. For more on this visit the informative website www.bettertrains4chepstow.co.uk

58 Newport Transporter Bridge

Location: Newport.
GPS: Newport: 51°35'20.10"N 2°59'37.09"W.
OS Map reference: Newport: ST318862.
Operator: Newport City Council.
Contact details: Newport City Council, Civic Centre, Newport, NP20 4UR. Telephone: 01633 656656.
E-mail: transporterbridge@newport.gov.uk
Route: From Usk Way (A4042) on the west bank to the Newport Transporter Road at Liswerry on the eastern side.
Journey time: The 645 ft between the towers is travelled at 10 ft per second.
Operating dates: Refurbishment work to the bridge began in early 2010 and was scheduled to last for around six months. Updates on progress will appear on www.newport.gov.uk/_dc/index.cfm?fuseaction=transporter.homepage When completed, the bridge will once again operate daily.
Comments: The Newport transporter bridge (w. *Pont Gludo Casnewydd*), majestically dominating the skyline, crosses an estuarial section of the River Usk at Newport. Whilst obviously not a 'railway' in the true sense, the engineering spectacle may well be of general interest to the reader. The ferry

platform, sometimes referred to as a 'gondola', carries up to six vehicles and 120 passengers on foot. It is suspended on wires which pass over wheels running on tracks moving the platform over the river from one station to the other. A direct current electricity supply provides the motive power for the crossing. It was designed and built by the French engineer Ferdinand Arnodin and opened in 1906. The structure is 177 ft high which allowed for the free passage of large sea vessels into the port. It is an outstanding and rare example of the transporter bridge concept of which only 23 have ever been built in the world, 11 of which have been demolished with others out of use. The service at Newport has been suspended indefinitely since the end of 2007. However, funding is available and renovation/repair is expected to be completed by the summer of 2010. When working again it will be one of only eight, of which it is the largest, still operational in the world. There are two others in Great Britain, one at Middlesbrough which is still working and one in Warrington which has been out of commission since 1964. There is another structure, the Royal Victoria Dock Bridge in London, which was built in 1998 and designed so it could be used as a transporter bridge but currently it is only used as a high-level footbridge. There was another structure near Warrington transporting traffic between Widnes and Runcorn. It was the first of its type in Britain and the largest ever built. It was dismantled in the early 1960s after the opening of a nearby suspension bridge. The Newport transporter bridge is Grade I listed.

What to see locally: The 14th century ruined Newport Castle is on the banks of the River Usk close to the transporter bridge and the railway bridge carrying the main line services from the Severn Tunnel and Chepstow. Located just outside Newport, on the road to Risca, is the Monmouthshire & Brecon Canal. There is a visitor centre at High Cross, manned by volunteers, which is close to a flight of 14 locks rising 160 ft over half a mile, it is an impressive sight. At Caerleon, four miles to the north-east of Newport city centre, was one of the most important military sites in Britain under the Roman Empire. It was the home to the 2nd Augustan Legion, housing at its peak some 5,000 soldiers and horsemen. There was an amphitheatre, baths, shops and temples. The remains of the amphitheatre and the barracks can be visited at any time of the year free of charge.

Comments: There is the active Friends of the Newport Transporter Bridge (FONTB) organisation run by volunteers (www.fontb.org.uk).

59 Dean Forest Railway

Location: Norchard, in Gloucestershire, about eight miles east of the Welsh border in England.

GPS: Norchard: 51°44′13.06″N 2°32′14.60″W. Lydney Junction: 51°43′6.75″N 2°31′49.80″W. Parkend: 51°46′4.97″N 2°33′24.69″W.

OS map references: Norchard SO627045. Lydney Junction: SO635020. Parkend: SO617080.

Operator: Dean Forest Railway Company Ltd.

Contact details: Dean Forest Railway, Norchard, Forest Road, Lydney, Gloucestershire GL15 4ET. Telephone: 01594 845840. A 24-hour information line is available on 01594 843423.
Route: Lydney Junction to Parkend via Norchard, a distance of four miles.
Journey time: Varies according to traction but about 30 minutes each way.
Gauge: Standard.
Traction: Includes a 1949-built pannier tank No. 9681 which spent most of its British Railways life operating at Tondu, Aberbeeg, Barry and Cardiff. It was withdrawn from service in 1965. It was rescued in 1975 and steamed again in 1984. Undergoing major overhaul are prairie tank No.5541, which hauled the first passenger train at Norchard and Hunslet 3806 *Wilbert*, both due for completion in 2010. The railway retains dmus: E50619 power car, M56492 trailer car, M59387 centre car, M51914 power car and M51566 power car. There is also a 1960-built Planet 0-4-0 No. 3947 used mainly on lineside clearance trains while shunting duties are currently shared between 0-4-0 diesel-hydraulic Hunslet 6688 *Salty* and a recently outshopped ex-BR class '08' No. 08238 *Charlie*. The *Royal Forester* dining car runs on many weekends offering four-course lunches and sometimes evening meals.
Website: www.deanforestrailway.co.uk

Lydney Junction station on 17th February, 2010, a very wet day!   *Author*

One of Dean Forest Railway's dmus awaits passengers at Parkend for the return journey to Lydney Junction on 17th February, 2010. *Author*

Operating dates: Services, both diesel and steam, are operated most months except January. Most weekends are covered from early April to early October as are some Sundays in February, March and October. Santa Specials run during the weekends running up to Christmas. Some other dates have services so it is well worth contacting the railway or visiting the helpful website before making a trip.

Tariff: Pay once and ride all day.

History of the line: In June 1810 horse-drawn vehicles began taking coal along a new tramroad between Parkend and Lydney and later expanded to the canal and harbour at Lydney, taking the name Severn & Wye Railway & Canal Company (S&W). In spite of the development of steam locomotion elsewhere in the early 19th century the S&W continued using horses until trials were undertaken using the 'new' traction in 1864 but the experiment surprisingly was deemed unsuccessful! Four years later a broad gauge railway was established alongside the tramroad but this was converted to standard gauge in 1872. By the time a further two years had elapsed the tramroad had largely fallen into disuse leaving only a local tin manufacturing enterprise to continue utilizing the route until 1883. In 1875, the S&W began to operate passenger services. On the opening of the Severn railway bridge in 1879, the S&W amalgamated with the Severn Bridge Railway Company. Passenger services to the north of Lydney Town were stopped in 1929, but trains to the south continued until the Severn bridge was closed by a maritime disaster in October 1960 (*see 'What to remember' entry below*). Lydney Town station was formally closed in 1964.

History of the heritage railway: The Dean Forest Railway Society, formed in 1970, operates in support of today's preserved railway. The aim was to safeguard the Lydney to Parkend branch line although British Rail at that time had not determined a date for closure. Its first Steam Open Day took place in October 1971 when a Peckett locomotive *Uskmouth I* delivered brake van rides over a short distance of 200 ft earning it at the time the rather unkind reputation as the 'World's Shortest Passenger Railway'! By 1973, British Rail still had not determined the future of the branch line so the society sought and acquired alternative accommodation at the former Norchard Colliery. Following much hard work the first open day was held there in 1978 on a 250 yard length of line. More track was laid extending the distance to 450 yards. Further extensions followed; first to Goatfield Curve, later to Thomas's Yard (just short of the main A48 level crossing) and, finally, in 1991, crossing the main road to terminate at St Mary's Halt. British Rail eventually decided to close the line in the early 1980s allowing the Dean Forest Railway, by the middle of that decade, to complete the purchase of most of the track and land. Later, part of the Lydney Junction site adjacent to the Gloucester to Newport/Cardiff main line was acquired. A subsequent successful application for a Light Railway Order allowed the completion of the link from Lydney Junction to Parkend. However, it was not until 1995 before the former Severn & Wye station at Lydney Junction could be opened to the first Dean Forest Railway passenger trains. Lydney Town station began operating in April 2001 and in December 2005 the lovingly restored Parkend station was re-opened allowing the first regular passenger trains to run again since closure in 1929.

What to remember locally: The Severn Bridge Disaster occurred during the late evening of 25th October, 1960. It occurred in thick fog when two tanker vessels on the river, the *Wastdale H* carrying petroleum spirit and the *Arkendale H* carrying fuel oil, missed the entrance to the docks and were swept up river by the incoming tide which was running at a speed of about eight knots. During attempts to find the dock entrance, the vessels either collided or ran alongside each other and were unable to separate. They were then swept against one of the piers of the three-quarter mile long railway bridge carrying the line between Lydney and Sharpness on the opposite bank. The impact carried away the pier causing two spans to fall, taking with them railway lines which fell across both vessels further locking them together. Both vessels had been so severely damaged that the contents of their tanks leaked into the river. It is understood that the petrol vapour from the *Wastdale H* ignited causing both vessels to catch fire with the flames at one time burning higher than the bridge. The mixture of burning petroleum spirit and fuel oil floated for one mile upstream until the ebb tide took it back towards the sea. As the blazing liquids reached the bridge the fire was spread over almost the whole width of the river. The vessels, still locked together, also floated upstream for about half a mile towards Gloucester before running aground on a sandbank. The disaster could have been much worse; the impact with the bridge had caused a 12 inch diameter gas main to be severed; fortunately the gas supply was switched off before it caught fire. The two vessels were in a very dangerous condition making salvage impossible. Five days later they were destroyed *in situ* by a series of small explosions. Five men, all sailors, lost their lives in the tragedy. More could have died for at the time of the collision some workers were employed on the bridge strengthening the spans. As their luck would have it, they had taken a break in the nearby signal box at Severn Bridge station in order to listen to a heavyweight boxing match on the radio involving Henry Cooper. The railway bridge was never repaired and it stood disused for several more years before being dismantled in the late 1960s.

What to see locally: Located between the Wye Valley (an Area of Outstanding Natural Beauty) and the River Severn is the Forest of Dean, England's first national forest park and its largest oak woodland. At Parkend, a short walk from the station, is the early 19th century Church of St Paul, the plan of which is interesting in that it is octagonal in shape. The church has a set of eight tubular bells which were installed as a memorial to those who lost their lives in World War I.

Neighbouring railways: Perrygrove Railway at Coleford is about three miles north-west of Parkend (*see below*). A Great Western Museum can also be found at Coleford in a corner of the Co-operative supermarket car park (*see entry 61*).

Comments: At Norchard there is shop and a static buffet car. The Dean Forest Railway Museum Trust also runs an interesting museum packed with relics of local railways, especially those from the former Severn & Wye Railway. Entry to the displays, through the shop, is free but donations are always appreciated. Enquiries from would-be volunteers to help with tasks on the railway are equally welcomed.

60 Perrygrove Railway

Location: Coleford, half a mile south on the B4228 road to Chepstow and three miles east of the Welsh border.
GPS: Perrygrove Railway: 51°47′15.71″N 2°36′48.56″W.
OS map references: Perrygrove: SO578959.
Operator: Treasure Train Ltd.
Contact details: Perrygrove Railway, Perrygrove Farm, Perrygrove Road, Coleford, Gloucestershire GL16 8QB. Telephone: 01594 834991. E-mail: website1@perrygrove.co.uk
Route: Perrygrove to Oakiron, a distance of three-quarters of a mile with two sections enjoying 1 in 30 gradients. A further quarter mile extension is planned for the future.
Journey time: A round trip of 24 minutes.
Gauge: Miniature (15 in.)
Traction: Steam locomotives - The Exmoor Steam Railway-built *Spirit of Adventure* completed in 1993. *Ursula* (Heywood recreation) built by James Waterfield. *Lydia* built by Alan Keef Ltd in 2008. Diesel locomotives include Simplex 26014/1963 *Workhorse* and Hunslet LD9337/1994 *Jubilee*.
Website: www.perrygrove.co.uk
Operating dates: Operating every Saturday, Sunday and Bank Holiday from Easter to Halloween, and every day in local school holidays. There are also some services operated in the run up to Christmas.
History: The railway was built by Michael and Frances Crofts and other enthusiastic volunteers on an old farm which had fallen into disrepair. The farm

The Perrygrove Railway's steam locomotive *Lydia*.   *Courtesy of the Perrygrove Railway*

The Perrygrove Railway's *Spirit of Adventure* with the treetop adventure houses in the background. *Courtesy of the Perrygrove Railway*

Ursula and the Perrygrove Railway's museum train. *Courtesy of the Perrygrove Railway*

was acquired in 1993 and planning permission granted a year later with ground-breaking taking place at Easter 1995. After much hard work the railway eventually opened to the public at the beginning of August 1996. In the process of development is the 'Treetop Adventure' which allows children to play in small houses among the trees.

Of related railway interest: The Perrygrove Railway is currently working on plans for a building to house the Heywood Collection. It was in about 1870 that Sir Arthur Percival Heywood, a graduate in mechanical engineering from Cambridge University, began experimenting to find the narrowest gauge 'possessing the necessary stability for practical use'. He eventually settled on 15 inches and completed his first locomotive of this gauge (*Effie*) in 1874. He worked at his home north of Derby and eventually developed a fine private railway with workshops. His experiments were put to practical use when, in 1896, the then Duke of Westminster commissioned Heywood to build a railway on the Grosvenor family's Eaton Estate at Chester on the English-Welsh border. A three-mile line was built linking the estate to Balderton on the Shrewsbury to Chester railway line which at that time was operated by the Great Western Railway. In all, the overall length of line amounted to 4½ miles. The Duke of the time estimated that the railway saved him £226 per year on road haulage costs, a significant sum in those days. The railway operated until 1946 with the track being lifted the following year. Some of the Eaton Hall rolling stock is now in the care of the Perrygrove Railway, notably the original saloon carriage. Whilst the original Eaton Hall Railway has long gone, the present Duke built the Eaton Park Railway in 1994. This railway runs a replica of the original 1896-built steam locomotive *Katie*. The railway is a totally private affair but can be viewed on one of the Grosvenor Estate's three garden open days during the year.

What to see locally: The Royal Forest of Dean.

Neighbouring railways: Dean Forest Railway is at Parkend three miles south-east of Coleford. A Great Western Railway Museum can also be found in Coleford.

61 Great Western Railway Museum at Coleford

Location: Coleford, just over the border in Gloucestershire, England.
GPS: Coleford: 51°47'38.16"N 2°36'58.26"W.
OS map reference: Coleford: SO577105.
Operator: The Great Western (Coleford) Museum.
Contact details: The Old Railway Station, Railway Drive, Coleford, GL16 8RH. Telephone: 01594 832032 (weekdays) and 01594 833569 (Saturdays). E-mail: coleford_gwr@yahoo.co.uk
Website: www.colefordgwr.150m.com
Operating dates: On Friday and Saturday afternoons from 1430 to 1700 hours.
The Museum: The Great Western Railway Museum, founded in 1988, is housed in one of the last remaining permanent railway buildings on the original site of Coleford railway yard. To be found there is the original Great Western Railway goods station of 1883 together with a Great Western signal box. On a short

The entrance to Coleford's Great Western Railway Museum. *Author*

GWR locomotive No. 6000 *King George V* standing at a typical GWR station built as a replica within the STEAM museum. *Author*

stretch of track stands the 1936-built Peckett 0-4-0ST locomotive No. 1893 together with ex-Great Western Railway rolling stock. There is also an LMS six-wheeled passenger brake coach, No. M32978, presently undergoing restoration at the East Lancashire Railway workshops. The museum traces the history of all the railways in the Forest of Dean from the early 1800s, when the first tracks were laid, up to the 1970s, when the heritage Dean Forest Railway was founded. The museum also retains information about the Wye Valley Railway, the Severn & Wye Railway and Monmouth Troy railway station. The museum also features scale models in 7¼ in., 5 in., 'O' and 'OO' gauges. Miniature steam locomotive rides are offered on some bank holidays. There is also an interesting collection of photographs of railways which operated in the Coleford and the Forest of Dean area. A Victorian ticket office, a goods office and station masters' office and a replica Victorian railway carriage can also be seen.
Comments: There is a shop and refreshments are available. Car parking nearby is free.

62 STEAM - Museum of the Great Western Railway

Location: Swindon, Wiltshire, England, 47 miles east of the border with South Wales.
GPS: Steam at Swindon: 51°34'40.07"N 1°48'6.60"W.
OS Map reference: Swindon: SU143848.
Operator: STEAM - Museum of the Great Western Railway.
Contact details: Steam, Kemble Drive, Swindon, SN2 2TA. Telephone: 01793 466 646. Fax: 01793 466 615 Textphone: 01793 466 618.
Website: www.steam-museum.org.uk
Operating dates: The museum and shop is open from 1000 to 1700 hours throughout the year. The last admission is 1630 hours.
The Museum: The award-winning 'STEAM, the Museum of the Great Western Railway' was opened in 2000 and is housed in a beautifully restored Grade II railway building in the heart of the former Swindon railway works. It is large with 70,000 square feet of displays. The museum tells the story of the men and women who built, operated and travelled on the Great Western Railway, a railway network that, through the pioneering vision and genius of Isambard Kingdom Brunel, was regarded as the most advanced in the world. This is an excellent, indeed absorbing, museum well worth visiting. For more information on what can be seen and events running, visit the comprehensive website.
Comments: The year 2010 marks the 175th anniversary of the creation of the Great Western Railway. A series of special events will take place across the region to celebrate this important milestone in railway history. Incidentally the museum can be looked on as a kind of crèche for the railway enthusiast whilst the 'shop to you drop' member(s) of the family can visit the adjacent Swindon Designer Outlet complex - in other words, something for all the family!

A recreation of the great man himself, Isambard Kingdom Brunel, in the STEAM Museum at Swindon standing in front of a replica of the broad gauge locomotive *North Star*.   *Author*

Glossary

Railway related Welsh language terms

Afon	River
Amserlen	Timetable
Canolog	Central, as in Cardiff Central
Cadw Seddi	Seat Reservations
Canol y Dref	Town centre
Cyffreddinol	General, as in Wrexham General
Cymorth	Assistance
Cwn a beiciau	Dogs and bicycles
Defnyddir locomotifau	Steam locomotive
Diesel locomotifau	Diesel locomotive
Dydd Llun i ddydd Gwener	Mondays to Fridays
Dydd Sarwrn	Saturdays
Dydd Sul	Sundays
Gorsaf	Station
Gwasanaethau trên hyd	Train services
Awyr	Airport
Plant	Children
Platfform	Platform
Pont	Bridge
Prisiau dwyffordd	Return fares
Rheilffordd	Railway
Siarter y Teithiwr	Passenger's Charter
Stryd Fawr	High Street
Trên	Train
Twnel	Tunnel
Y dosbarth cyntaf	First class travel

List of Welsh town/village names with main line railway stations

Aberdâr	Aberdare
Aberdaugleddau	Milford Haven
Aberdyfi	Aberdovey
Abermaw	Barmouth
Aberpennar	Mountain Ash
Abertawe	Swansea
Abertyleri	Abertillery
Arberth	Narberth
Bae Caerdydd	Cardiff Bay
Bae Colwyn	Colwyn Bay
Bwcle	Buckley
Bynie	Bynea
Caerdydd	Cardiff
Caerdydd Heol y Frenhines	Cardiff Queen Street
Caerffilli	Caerphilly
Caerfyrddin	Carmarthen
Caergybi	Holyhead
Cas-gwent	Chepstow
Casnewydd	Newport
Castell-nedd	Neath
Cilgeti	Kilgetty
Conwy	Conway
Cydweli	Kidwelly
Cyff Dyfi	Dovey Junction
Cyffordd Twnel Hafren	Severn Tunnel Junction

185

Dinbych-y-Pysgod	Tenby
Dociau'r Barri	Barry Dock
Ffestiniog	Festiniog
Ffynnon Taf	Taffs Well
Glanyfferi	Ferryside
Glyn Ebwy	Ebbw Vale
Hendy-gwyn	Whitland
Heol Dingle	Dingle Road
Hwlffordd	Haverfordwest
Cnwclas	Knucklas
Landyfal	Lamphey
Llanhiedd	Llanhilleth
Llansawel	Briton Ferry
Llaniltud Fawr	Llanwit Major
Llanymddyfi	Llandovery
Llysfaen	Lisvane
Llwynbedw	Birchgrove
Maenorbyr	Manorbier
Merthyr Tudful	Merthyr Tydfil
Mynwent y Crynwyr	Quakers Yard
Pembre	Pembrey
Penarlag	Hawarden
Penalun	Penally
Penfro	Pembroke
Pen-y-Bont	Bridgend
Pontllottyn	Pontlottyn
Pont Rufeinig	Roman Bridge
Pontypwl	Pontypool
Porthladd Abergwaun	Fishguard Harbour
Porth Tywyn	Burry Port
Rhisga	Risca
Rhiwabon	Ruabon
Rhws	Roose
Rhydaman	Ammanford
Rhymni	Rhymney
Sgiwen	Skewen
Trecelyn	Newbridge
Trefyclawdd	Knighton
Tregatwg	Cadoxton
Tre-Gwyr	Gowerton
Treorci	Treochy
Wrecsam	Wrexham
Y Barri	Barry
Y Drenewydd	Newtown
Y Fali	Valley
Y Fenni	Abergavenny
Y Fflint	Flint
Y Pil	Pyle
Y Trallwng	Welshpool
Y Ty Du	Rogerstone
Y Tyllgoed	Fairwater
Y Waun	Chirk
Ynys Barri	Barry Island
Ynys Môn	Isle of Anglesey
Yr Eglwys Newydd	Whitchurch
Yr Hob	Hope
Ystrad Trefforest	Trefforest Estate

Useful Sources

Websites

Arriva Trains Wales	www.arrivatrainswales.co.uk
Author's Website	www.rail-guides.eu
Welsh Castles	www.castlewales.com
Cross Country Trains	www.crosscountrytrains.co.uk
Cycle Routes, National	www.sustrans.org.uk
First Great Western	www.firstgreatwestern.co.uk
Great Little Trains of Wales	www.greatlittletrainsofwales.co.uk
Great Western Archive	www.greatwestern.org.uk
Great Western Society, Didcot	www.didcotrailwaycentre.org.uk
National Railway Museum	www.nrm.org.uk
Oakwood Press, The	www.oakwoodpress.co.uk
Railway ramblers	www.railwayramblers.org.uk
Steam Museum, Swindon	www.steam-museum.org.uk
UK Heritage Railways	http://ukhrail.uel.ac.uk
UK Steam Tours information	www.uksteam.info
Virgin Trains	www.virgintrains.co.uk
Wales Guide	www.walesdirectory.co.uk.
Wales Rails	www.walesrails.co.uk
Welsh Assembly	http://wales.gov.uk/
Welsh Icons	www.welshicons.org.uk
Welsh Railways Research Circle	www.wrrc.org.uk/
Welsh Tourism	www.visitwales.co.uk
Wrexham & Shropshire	www.wrexhamandshropshire.co.uk

Addresses

Arriva Trains Wales, St Mary's House, Penarth, Cardiff CF10 5DJ. Telephone: 08457 48 49 50 (booking enquiries). General enquiries: 029 20 720 500.
Cross Country Trains is part of the Arriva Group.
First Great Western, First Great Western, Plymouth, PL4 6ZZ. Telephone: 08457 000 125 (customer services, telesales and lost property).
Great Little Trains of Wales, FREEPOST CS1226, Wharf Station, Tywyn, Gwynedd, LL36 9BR.
The Oakwood Press, PO Box 13, Usk, Monmouthshire, NP15 1YS. Telephone: 01291 650444. Fax: 01291 650484. E-mail: sales@oakwoodpress.co.uk
Virgin Trains, Customer Relations, PO Box 713, Birmingham, B5 4HH. Telephone: 08450 008 000. Text phone: 01216 547 528.
Welsh Tourism, Welsh Assembly Government, Cardiff Bay. Telephone: 08708 300 306 Fax: 08701 211259. Minicom: 08701 211255. Email: info@visitwales.co.uk
Wrexham & Shropshire Railway, Great Central House, Marylebone Station, Melcombe Place, London, NW1 6JJ. And at The Pump House, Coton Hill, Shrewsbury, SY1 2DP. Telephone: 0845 260 5900 (telesales) and 0845 260 5200 (customer comments).

Welsh Tourist Information Centres

North Wales

North Wales Tourism - Head Office, 77 Conwy Road, Colwyn Bay, LL29 7LN. Tel: 01492 531731. Fax: 01492 530059. Email: croeso@nwt.co.uk Web: http://www.nwt.co.uk/
Aberdyfi - The Wharf Gardens, Aberdyfi, LL35 0ED. Tel: 01654 767 321. Fax: 01654 767 321. Email: tic.aberdyfi@eryri-npa.gov.uk
Bala - Penllyn, Pensarn Road, Bala, LL23 7SR. Tel: 01678 521 021. Fax: 01678 521 021 Email: bala.tic@gwynedd.gov.uk
Bangor - Town Hall, Ffordd Deiniol, Bangor, LL57 2RE. Tel: 01248 352786. Fax: 01248 352786. Email: bangor.tic@gwynedd.gov.uk
Barmouth - The Station, Station Road, Barmouth, LL42 1LU. Tel: 01341 280 787. Fax: 01341 280 787. Email: barmouth.tic@gwynedd.gov.uk
Beddgelert - Canolfan Hebog, Beddgelert, LL55 4YD. Tel: 01766 890615. Fax: 01766 890615. Email: tic.beddgelert@eryri-npa.gov.uk
Betws-y-Coed - Tourist Information Centre , Royal Oak Stables, Betws-y-Coed, Conwy, LL24 0AH. Tel: 01690 710426. Fax: 01690 710665. Email: tic.byc@eryri-npa.gov.uk
Blaenau Ffestiniog - Unit 3, High Street, Blaenau Ffestiniog, LL41 3ES. Tel: 01766 830 360. Fax: 01766 830 360. Email: tic.blaenau@eryri-npa.gov.uk
Caernarfon - Oriel Pendeitsh, Castle Street, Caernarfon, LL55 1ES. Tel: 01286 672 232. Fax: 01286 676 476. Email: caernarfon.tic@gwynedd.gov.uk
Conwy - Conwy Castle Visitor Centre, Conwy Castle, Conwy, LL32 8LD. Tel: 01492 592248. Fax: 01492 573545. Email: conwytic@conwy.gov.uk
Dolgellau - Ty Meirion, Eldon Square, Dolgellau, LL40 1PU.Tel: 01341 422888. Fax: 01341 422576. Email: tic.dolgellau@eryri-npa.gov.uk
Harlech - Llys y Graig, High Street, Harlech, LL46 2YE. Tel: 01766 780 658. Fax: 01766 780 658. Email: tic.harlech@eryri-npa.gov.uk
Holyhead - Stena Line, Terminal 1, Holyhead, Isle of Anglesey, LL65 1DQ. Tel: 01407 762622. Fax: 01407 761462. Email: holyhead@nwtic.com
Llanberis - 41b High Street, Llanberis, LL55 4EU. Tel: 01286 870 765. Fax: 01286 871 924. Email: llanberis.tic@gwynedd.gov.uk
Llandudno - Library Building, Mostyn Street, Llandudno, LL30 2RP. Tel: 01492 577 577. Fax: 01492 577 578. Email: llandudnotic@conwy.gov.uk
Llanfairpwllgwyngyll - Station Site, Llanfairpwllgwyngyll, Isle of Anglesey, LL61 5UJ. Tel: 01248 713177. Fax: 01248 715711. Email: llanfairpwll@nwtic.com
Llangollen - Y Chapel, Castle Street, Llangollen, LL20 8NU. Tel: 01978 860828. Fax: 01978 861563. Email: llangollen@nwtic.com
Mold - Library, Museum & Art Gallery, Earl Road, Mold, Flintshire, CH7 1AP. Tel: 01352 759 331. Fax: 01352 759 331. Email: mold@nwtic.com
Porthmadog - High Street, Porthmadog, LL49 9LD. Tel: 01766 512981. Fax: 01766 515312. Email: porthmadog.tic@gwynedd.gov.uk
Pwllheli - Min y Don, Station Square, Pwllheli, LL53 5HG. Tel: 01758 613000. Fax: 01758 613000. Email: pwllheli.tic@gwynedd.gov.uk
Rhyl - Rhyl Children's Village, West Parade, Rhyl, Denbighshire, LL18 1HZ. Tel: 01745 355068. Fax: 01745 342255. Email: rhyl.tic@denbighshire.gov.uk
Tywyn - High Street, Tywyn, LL36 9AD. Tel: 01654 710 070. Fax: 01654 710 070 Email: tywyn.tic@gwynedd.gov.uk
Wrexham - Lambpit Street, Wrexham, LL11 1WN. Tel: 01978 292015. Fax: 01978 292 467. Email: tic@wrexham.gov.uk

Mid Wales

Aberaeron - The Quay, Aberaeron, Ceredigion, Dyfed, SA46 0BT. Tel: 01545 570602. Fax: 01545 571534. Email: aberaerontic@ceredigion.gov.uk

Aberystwyth - Terrace Road, Aberystwyth, Ceredigion, Dyfed, SY23 2AG. Tel: 01970 612125. Fax: 01970 612125 Email: aberystwythtic@ceredigion.gov.uk

Borth - Cambrian Terrace, Borth, Ceredigion, Dyfed, SY24 5HY. Tel: 01970 871 174. Fax: 01970 871 365 Email: borthtic@ceredigion.gov.uk

Brecon - Cattle Market Car Park, Brecon, Powys, LD3 9DA. Tel: 01874 622 485. Fax: 01874 625 256. Email: brectic@powys.gov.uk

Brecon Beacons National Park - The Mountain Centre, Libanus, Brecon, Powys, LD3 7DP. Tel: 01874 623 366.

Builth Wells - The Groe Car Park, Builth Wells, Powys, LD2 3BL. Tel: 01982 553 307. Fax: 01982 553 841. Email: builtic@powys.gov.uk

Cardigan - Theatr Mwldan, Bath House Road, Cardigan, Ceredigion, Dyfed, SA43 1JY. Tel: 01239 613 230. Fax: 01239 614 853. Email: cardigantic@ceridigion.gov.uk

Knighton - Offa's Dyke Centre, West Street, Knighton, Powys, LD7 1EN. Tel: 01547 528 753. Fax: 01547 529 027 Email: oda@offasdyke.demon.co.uk

Llanidloes - Customer Service Point, Mount Street, Llanidloes, Powys, SY18 6EY. Tel: 01686 412 855. Email: cspllanidloes@powys.gov.uk

Machynlleth - Royal House, Penrallt Street, Machynlleth, Powys, SY20 8AG. Tel: 01654 702 401.Fax: 01654 703 675. Email: mactic@powys.gov.uk

New Quay - Church Street, New Quay, Ceredigion, Dyfed, SA45 9NZ. Tel: 01545 560 865. Fax: 01545 561 360. Email: newquaytic@ceredigion.gov.uk

Newtown -The Park, Back Lane, Newtown, Powys, SY16 2NH. Tel: 01686 625 580. Fax: 01686 610 066. Email: newtic@powys.gov.uk

Presteigne -The Judge's Lodging, Broad Street, Presteigne, Powys, LD8 2AD. Tel: 01544 260 650. Fax: 01544 260 652. Email: presteignetic@powys.gov.uk

Rhayader - The Leisure Centre, North Street, Rhayader, Powys, LD6 5BU. Tel: 01597 810591. Email: rhayader.tic@powys.gov.uk

Welshpool - Vicarage Garden, Church Street, Welshpool, Powys, SY21 7DD. Tel: 01938 552043. Fax: 01938 554 038. Email: ticwelshpool@btconnect.com

South Wales

Aberdulais Falls - Aberdulais Falls National Trust property, Aberdulais, Neath, SA10 8EU. Tel: 01639 636 674 Fax: 01639 645 069. Email: aberdulaistic@nationaltrust.org.uk

Abergavenny - Swan Meadow, Monmouth Road, Abergavenny, NP7 5HH. Tel : 01873 857588. Fax: 01873 850217. Email: abergavenny-tic@tsww.com

Barry Island - The Promenade, The Triangle, Barry Island, CF62 5TQ. Tel: 01446 747 171. Fax: 01446 747 171. Email: barrytic@valeofglamorgan.gov.uk

Blaenavon - Blaenavon World Heritage Centre, Church Road, Blaenavon, Torfaen, NP4 9AS. Tel: 01495 742 333. Fax: 01495 742 332. Email: blaenavon.tic@torfaen.gov.uk

Bridgend - McArthurGlen Designer Outlet Village, The Derwen, Bridgend, CF32 9SU. Tel: 01656 654906. Fax: 01656 646523. Email: bridgendtic@bridgend.gov.uk

Caerleon - 5 High Street, Caerleon, NP18 1AE. Tel: 01633 422 656. Fax: 01633 422 656 Email: caerleon.tic@newport.gov.uk

Caerphilly - Lower Twyn Square, Caerphilly, CF83 1JL. Tel: 029 2088 0011. Fax: 029 2086 0811. Email: tourism@caerphilly.gov.uk

Cardiff - The Old Library, The Hayes, Cardiff, CF10 1AH. Tel: 029 20873 573. Fax: 029 2023 2058. Email: visitor@cardiff.gov.uk

Carmarthen - 113 Lammas Street, Carmarthen, Carmarthenshire, SA31 3AQ. Tel: 01267 231 557. Fax: 01267 221 901. Email: carmarthentic@carmarthenshire.gov.uk

Chepstow - Castle Car Park, Bridge Street, Chepstow, NP16 5EY. Tel: 01291 623772. Fax: 01291 628004. Email: chepstow.tic@monmouthshire.gov.uk

Crickhowell - Beaufort Chambers, Beaufort Street, Crickhowell, NP8 1AA. Tel : 01873 812105. cricktic@powys.gov.uk

Fishguard - Town Hall, Market Square, Fishguard, SA65 9HA. Tel: 01437 776 636. Fax: 01348 875 582. Email: fishguard.tic@pembrokeshire.gov.uk

Fishguard Harbour - Ocean Lab, The Parrog, Goodwick, Fishguard, Pembrokeshire, SA64 0DE. Tel: 01348 872 037. Fax: 01348 872 528. Email: fishguardharbour.tic@pembrokeshire.gov.uk

Haverfordwest - 19 Old Bridge, Haverfordwest, Pembrokeshire, SA61 2EZ. Tel: 01437 763110. Fax: 01437 767738. Email: haverfordwest.tic@pembrokeshire.gov.uk

Hay-on-Wye - Oxford Road, Hay-on-Wye, HR3 5DG. Tel: 01497 820144. Fax: 01497 820015.

Llandeilo - Car Park, Crescent Road, Llandeilo, SA19 6HN. Tel : 01558 824226. Fax: 01558 824252.

Llandovery - Heritage Centre, Kings Road, Llandovery, Carmarthenshire, SA20 0AW. Tel: 01550 720693. Fax: 01550 720693. Email: llandovery.ic@breconbeacons.org

Llanelli - Millennium Coastal Park Visitor Centre, North Dock, Llanelli, Carmarthenshire, SA15 2LF. Tel: 01554 777 744. Fax: 01554 757 825. Email: DiscoveryCentre@carmarthenshire.gov.uk

Llanwrtyd Wells -Ty Barcud, The Square, Llanwrtyd Wells, LD5 4RB. Tel : 01591 610666. Fax: 01591 610666.

Merthyr Tydfil - 14a Glebeland Street, Merthyr Tydfil, CF47 8AU. Tel: 01685 379 884. Fax: 01685 379 884. Email: tic@merthyr.gov.uk

Milford Haven - Suite 19, Cedar Court, Milford Haven, Pembrokeshire, SA73 3LS. Tel: 01437 771 818. Email: milford.tic@pembrokeshire.gov.uk

Monmouth - Shire Hall, Agincourt Square, Monmouth, NP5 3DY. Tel: 01600 713899. Fax: 01600 772794. Email: monmouth.tic@monmouthshire.gov.uk

Mumbles - Mumbles Methodist Church, Mumbles Road, Mumbles, Swansea, SA3 4BU. Tel: 01792 361302. Fax: 01792 363392. Email: info@mumblestic.co.uk
Web: http://www.mumblestic.co.uk

Newport (Dyfed) - 2 Bank Cottages, Long Street, Newport, Pembrokeshire, SA42 0TN. Tel: 01239 820 912. Fax: 01239 821 258. Email: NewportTIC@pembrokeshirecoast.org.uk

Newport (Gwent) - Museum & Art Gallery, John Frost Square, Newport, NP20 1PA. Tel: 01633 842962. Fax: 01633 222615. Email: newport.tic@newport.gov.uk

Pembroke - Visitor Centre, Commons Road, 38 Main Street, Pembroke, Pembrokeshire, SA71 4EA. Tel: 01437 776499. Email: pembroke.tic@pembrokeshire.gov.uk

Penarth - Penarth Pier, The Esplanade, Penarth, CF64 3AU. Tel: 029 2070 8849. Email: penarthtic@valeofglamorgan.gov.uk

Pontypridd - Pontypridd Museum, Bridge Street, Pontypridd, Rhondda Cynon Taff, CF37 4PE. Tel: 01443 490 748. Fax: 01443 490 746. Email: tourism@pontypriddmuseum.org.uk

Pont Nedd Fechan - Pont Nedd Fechan, Nr Glynneath, SA11 5NR. Tel : 01639 721795.

Porthcawl - Old Police Station, John Street, Porthcawl, Bridgend, CF36 3DT. Tel: 01656 786 639. Fax: 01656 782 387. Email: porthcawltic@bridgend.gov.uk

Saundersfoot - Barbecue, Harbour Car Park, Saundersfoot, Pembrokeshire, SA69 9HE. Tel: 01834 813672. Fax: 01834 813673. Email: saundersfoot.tic@pembrokeshire.gov.uk

St David's - Orie Y Parc, St David's, Pembrokeshire, SA62 6NW. Tel: 01437 720 392. Email: enquiries@stdavids.pembrokeshirecoast.org.uk

Swansea - Plymouth Street, Swansea, SA1 3QG. Tel: 01792 468 321. Fax: 01792 464 602. Email: tourism@swansea.gov.uk

Talgarth - The Tower Shop, Talgarth, LD3 0BW. Tel: 01874 712 226. Fax: 0870 0542916.

Tenby - Unit 2, The Gateway Complex, Tenby, SA70 7LT. Tel: 01834 842 402. Fax: 01834 845 439. Email: tenby.tic@pembrokeshire.gov.uk

Bibliography

Essential Guide to French Heritage & Tourist Railways, The. The Oakwood Press, Usk, 2006 ISBN: 978 85361 648 1.
Essential Guide to Swiss Heritage & Tourist Railways, The. The Oakwood Press, Usk, 2007 ISBN: 978 85361 659 7.
Essential Guide to Austrian Railways & Tramways, The. The Oakwood Press, Usk, 2008 ISBN: 978 85361 674 0.
Pictorial Guide to Alpine Railways, A. The Oakwood Press, Usk, 2009 ISBN: 978 85361 690 0.
Llanelly & Mynydd Mawr Railway by M.R.C. Price. Oakwood Press, 1992. ISBN 0 85361 423 7 and ISBN 978 0 85361 423 4.
Ordnance Survey Maps used were in the Landranger series 1:50 000 scale (2 cm to 1 km [1.25 inches to 1 mile]).
Nos. 114 Anglesey, 115 Snowdon, 116 Denbigh & Colwyn Bay, 117 Chester & Wrexham, 124 Dolgellau, 125 Bala & Lake Vyrnwy, 126 Shrewsbury, 135 Aberystwyth & Machynlleth, 137 Church Stretton & Ludlow, 146 Lampeter & Llandovery, 147, Elan Valley & Builth Wells, 157 St David's & Haverfordwest, 158 Tenby & Pembroke, 159 Swansea & Gower, 160 Brecon Beacons, 161 The Black Mountains, 170 Vale of Glamorgan, and 171 Cardiff & Newport.
Rail Atlas - Great Britain & Ireland by S.K. Baker. Oxford Publishing Company, 2001. ISBN 0 86093 553 1.
Remembrance of a Riot: the story of the Llanelli Railway Strike Riots of 1911 by John Edwards (Llanelli Borough Council, 1988). This can be accessed in the Cardiff Central Library under the reference: *Astudiaethau Lleol*/Local Studies S 10).
The Swansea Valley Railway and how it moved to Bronwydd by Iain Pearce published in the Gwili Messenger No. 115 Winter 2009.

Photographic information

During the course of the preparation of this book 3,813 images were taken by the author and his wife between 2004 and 2010 with the majority shot in 2009 and 2010. Nikon digital cameras were used exclusively: viz, DX models -D100, D70, D200, D300 and FX model - D700. Lenses used, again all Nikon/Nikkor, were AF 50mm 1.8D FX, AF-S 18-70mm 3.5-4.5 DX, VR AF-S 18-200mm 3.-5.6G ED DX,AF 24-85mm 2.8-4D MACRO FX, AF 28-200mm 3.5-5.6D FX, 70-300mm 4-5.6 ED FX and VR 80-400mm 4.5-5.6ED FX. Nikon's dedicated flashgun model SB800 was also used from time to time. A Manfrotto 005 tripod, a gorillapod and a 'bean-bag' pod were used in support. As an aid to the author or his wife to remember exactly where they were when the photographs were taken a Nikon GP1 and/or Jobo photoGPS were used to embed GPS information in the individual metadata files. All photographs were shot in Nikon RAW format (NEF) and processed using Adobe Photoshop CS4, Nikon NX2 software and Adobe Lightroom 3 (beta). Picture files, in CMYK colour representation for printing, were saved to TIFF format.

Index